Start a Business
Like a Pro

A Complete solution to all Business start-up challenges.

J. R. Fried

Neon Books

Table of Contents

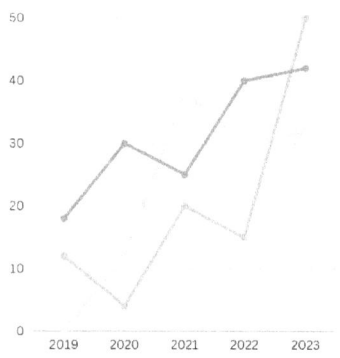 

S tarting a business is an exciting and challenging endeavor that requires careful planning and execution. Whether you have a unique product or service idea, a passion for entrepreneurship, or a desire to be your own boss, launching a business can be a rewarding experience. Here's an introduction to the key aspects of starting a business:

1. **Idea and Concept Development:**
    - Start by identifying a business idea or concept that you are passionate about and that addresses a specific problem or meets a need in the market.
    - Conduct market research to assess the demand for your product or service and understand your target audience.
2. **Business Plan:**
    - Create a comprehensive business plan outlining your business goals, strategies, financial projections, and operational plans.
    - A well-structured business plan is essential for obtaining financing, attracting investors, and guiding your business's growth.
3. **Legal Structure:**
    - Choose a legal structure for your business, such as sole proprietorship, partnership, LLC (Limited Liability Company), or corporation.

- Each structure has its own legal and tax implications, so consult with legal and financial professionals to make the right choice.

4. **Business Name and Registration:**
   - Select a unique and memorable business name and check its availability to ensure it's not already in use.
   - Register your business name with the appropriate government authorities and obtain any necessary licenses or permits.

5. **Financing:**
   - Determine how you'll finance your startup. This can include personal savings, loans, grants, or seeking investment from venture capitalists or angel investors.
   - Create a detailed budget and financial plan to manage your startup costs and ongoing expenses.

6. **Location and Infrastructure:**
   - Decide on the location for your business, whether it's a physical storefront, an office, or an online operation.
   - Set up the necessary infrastructure, such as equipment, technology, and facilities.

7. **Branding and Marketing:**
   - Develop a strong brand identity, including a logo, tagline, and brand message.
   - Create a marketing plan that outlines how you'll reach and engage with your target customers through advertising, social media, and other channels.

8. **Operations and Management:**
   - Define your business's operational processes and workflows.
   - Determine your management structure and roles within the company.

9. **Legal and Regulatory Compliance:**
   - Ensure your business complies with all local, state, and federal regulations, including tax requirements, employment laws, and industry-specific regulations.

10. **Launch and Growth:**
    - Plan a launch strategy to introduce your product or service to the market.
    - Continuously assess and adapt your business based on customer feedback and market changes to foster growth and sustainability.

11. Financial Management:
- Keep meticulous financial records and monitor your cash flow to ensure the financial health of your business.
- Consider seeking the advice of an accountant or financial advisor to help with financial management.

12. Customer Service:
- Provide excellent customer service to build a loyal customer base and generate positive word-of-mouth referrals.

13. Adaptability and Learning:
- Be prepared to adapt to changing market conditions and learn from your successes and failures as you grow your business.

Starting a business is a dynamic journey that requires dedication, resilience, and continuous learning. Surround yourself with a support network of mentors, advisors, and peers who can provide guidance and encouragement along the way. Keep in mind that while entrepreneurship can be challenging, it also offers the opportunity to turn your vision into reality and make a positive impact on your customers and community.

Why Start a Business?

Starting a business can be a rewarding and fulfilling endeavor for a variety of reasons. Here are some common motivations behind why people choose to start their own businesses:

1. **Independence and Autonomy:**
   - Many entrepreneurs desire the freedom to be their own boss and make decisions independently. Running a business allows you to set your own direction and priorities.

2. **Passion and Personal Fulfillment:**
   - Starting a business often stems from a deep passion for a particular product, service, or industry. It allows individuals to pursue their interests and do what they love.

3. **Financial Potential:**
   - Entrepreneurship can provide the potential for significant financial rewards. Successful businesses can generate profits and wealth for their owners.

4. **Innovation and Creativity:**

- Entrepreneurs have the opportunity to innovate and create new solutions, products, or services that address market needs or problems.

5. **Control Over Work-Life Balance:**
   - Many entrepreneurs seek a better work-life balance and the flexibility to set their own work hours, which can be especially important for those with families or personal commitments.

6. **Job Security:**
   - Some individuals start businesses as a response to job insecurity or a desire for greater job stability. Owning a business can provide a sense of control over one's financial future.

7. **Impact and Contribution:**

   - Entrepreneurs often want to make a positive impact on their communities or the world. Starting a business can be a means to address social, environmental, or humanitarian issues.

8. **Legacy and Family Business:**
   - Some entrepreneurs start businesses with the intention of creating a legacy or passing down a family tradition. Family-owned businesses can have deep cultural and personal significance.

9. **Learning and Growth:**
   - Entrepreneurship is a continuous learning experience. Many people are drawn to the opportunity to expand their skills and knowledge in various aspects of business.

10. **Challenge and Adventure:**
    - Entrepreneurship can be an exciting and challenging adventure. Overcoming obstacles, taking calculated risks, and achieving milestones can be personally fulfilling.

11. **Community Engagement:**
    - Owning a business can connect you to your local community and provide opportunities to engage with customers, partners, and other business owners.

12. **Job Creation:**
    - Entrepreneurship contributes to job creation, which can have a positive economic impact on a region or country. Many

entrepreneurs take pride in providing employment opportunities.

13. **Economic and Wealth Building:**
    - Building a successful business can be a pathway to wealth creation and financial security, not only for the owner but also for employees and stakeholders.

It's important to note that entrepreneurship comes with its share of challenges, risks, and uncertainties. Not all businesses succeed, and the road to success can be arduous. Therefore, individuals should carefully evaluate their motivations, prepare thoroughly, and seek mentorship and support when embarking on their entrepreneurial journey. Ultimately, the reasons for starting a business can be deeply personal, and they can evolve over time as the business grows and changes.

The Entrepreneurial Mindset

The entrepreneurial mindset refers to a particular way of thinking and approaching opportunities, challenges, and decision-making that is characteristic of successful entrepreneurs. This mindset is not limited to business owners but can also be applied in various aspects of life. Here are some key elements of the entrepreneurial mindset:

1. **Risk-Taking:**
   - Entrepreneurs are willing to take calculated risks. They understand that innovation and growth often require stepping outside of one's comfort zone and accepting the possibility of failure.
2. **Opportunity Recognition:**
   - Entrepreneurs have a keen ability to identify opportunities in the market or within existing systems. They see problems as opportunities to find creative solutions.
3. **Problem-Solving:**
   - An entrepreneurial mindset involves a problem-solving orientation. Entrepreneurs approach challenges as puzzles to be solved, using creativity and resourcefulness to find solutions.
4. **Adaptability:**
   - Entrepreneurs are adaptable and open to change. They recognize that markets, technology, and circumstances evolve, and they are willing to pivot and adjust their strategies accordingly.

5. **Resilience:**
   - The entrepreneurial mindset includes resilience in the face of setbacks and failures. Entrepreneurs understand that setbacks are part of the process and use them as learning experiences.
6. **Self-Confidence:**
   - Entrepreneurs have confidence in their abilities and ideas. This self-belief is often essential when facing skepticism or criticism from others.
7. **Vision and Goal Orientation:**
   - Entrepreneurs have a clear vision of what they want to achieve. They set specific goals and create strategies to work toward those goals.
8. **Resourcefulness:**
   - An entrepreneurial mindset involves resourcefulness, the ability to make the most of available resources and find creative solutions, even when resources are limited.
9. **Proactiveness:**
   - Entrepreneurs are proactive individuals who take initiative and are not content with the status quo. They are driven to make things happen.
10. **Networking and Relationship Building:**
    - Entrepreneurs understand the value of building a strong network of contacts and relationships. They seek opportunities for collaboration and partnership.
11. **Passion and Drive:**
    - Passion is a driving force for entrepreneurs. They are often deeply passionate about their ideas or businesses, and this passion fuels their determination and perseverance.
12. **Continuous Learning:**
    - Entrepreneurs have a growth mindset and are committed to lifelong learning. They actively seek knowledge and seek to improve themselves and their businesses.
13. **Customer-Centric Focus:**
    - Entrepreneurs prioritize understanding their customers' needs and providing value. They are attentive to feedback and strive to exceed customer expectations.
14. **Financial Literacy:**

- Entrepreneurs possess financial acumen and understand the importance of managing finances wisely. They monitor budgets, cash flow, and financial metrics.

15. Ethical and Responsible Behavior:
- Many successful entrepreneurs operate with a strong sense of ethics and responsibility, recognizing the impact of their actions on society, the environment, and their stakeholders.

Developing an entrepreneurial mindset is not something that happens overnight; it's a continuous process of growth and self-improvement. It involves cultivating these characteristics and applying them in various situations, whether you're starting a business, pursuing a career, or addressing personal goals. Ultimately, the entrepreneurial mindset empowers individuals to navigate uncertainty, seize opportunities, and create positive change in their lives and the world around them.

The Road Ahead

"The road ahead" is a phrase often used to describe the future or the path that lies ahead of an individual, organization, or society. It implies a journey or a forward-looking perspective. The road ahead is uncertain and can be influenced by a variety of factors, but planning and preparation are essential for navigating it successfully. Here are some key considerations related to "the road ahead":

1. Vision and Goals:
- Clearly define your vision for the future and set specific goals that you want to achieve. Your goals provide direction and purpose as you move forward.

2. Planning:
- Develop a strategic plan that outlines the steps and strategies needed to reach your goals. A well-thought-out plan can help you make informed decisions and allocate resources effectively.

3. Adaptability:
- The road ahead is unpredictable, and circumstances may change. Being adaptable and open to adjustments in your plans is crucial for dealing with unexpected challenges or opportunities.

4. Continuous Learning:

- The journey ahead often requires acquiring new knowledge and skills. Embrace opportunities for learning and personal growth to stay relevant and competitive.

5. **Resilience:**
   - Challenges and setbacks are inevitable. Cultivate resilience to bounce back from adversity and maintain your commitment to your goals.

6. **Resource Management:**
   - Efficiently manage your resources, whether they are financial, time, or human resources. Effective resource management is key to achieving your objectives.

7. **Risk Management:**
   - Identify potential risks and develop strategies to mitigate them. Risk management helps you navigate uncertainty with greater confidence.

8. **Innovation and Creativity:**
   - Innovation can open up new paths and opportunities. Encourage creativity and explore novel solutions to problems or challenges you may encounter.

9. **Networking and Collaboration:**
   - Building relationships and collaborating with others can provide support and open doors to new possibilities. Networking is valuable on the road ahead.

10. **Monitoring and Evaluation:**
   - Regularly assess your progress toward your goals. Monitoring and evaluation enable you to make adjustments and stay on track.

11. **Ethical Considerations:**
   - Maintain ethical and responsible behavior as you move forward. Ethical conduct builds trust and credibility in your journey.

12. **Sustainability and Responsibility:**
   - Consider the long-term impact of your actions on the environment, society, and future generations. Sustainability and social responsibility are increasingly important aspects of the road ahead.

13. **Flexibility:**

- Be prepared to pivot or change course if circumstances warrant it. Flexibility in your approach can help you navigate unexpected turns.

14. Long-Term Perspective:

- While short-term goals are important, also keep a long-term perspective in mind. Think about how your actions today will affect your future journey.

15. Balance and Well-Being:

- Ensure that you maintain a healthy work-life balance and take care of your physical and mental well-being. Your personal health and happiness are crucial on the road ahead.

The road ahead is different for everyone, shaped by individual goals, circumstances, and choices. Whether you are embarking on a new career, starting a business, pursuing personal aspirations, or facing significant life changes, a thoughtful and strategic approach can help you navigate the path ahead with confidence and resilience. Remember that the journey is as important as the destination, and each step you take contributes to your growth and development.

F inding a viable business idea is an exciting and important step in starting your own venture. Here are some steps to help you identify and develop a business idea that suits your interests, skills, and market needs:

1. **Self-Assessment:**
   - Identify your passions, interests, and areas of expertise. Consider what you enjoy doing in your free time or the skills you've developed over the years.
   - Assess your strengths and weaknesses. What are you good at, and where might you need support or improvement?
   - Determine your financial and time constraints. How much capital and time can you invest in your business idea?
2. **Market Research:**
   - Identify market trends and gaps. Research industries and markets that interest you to find out where there might be unmet needs or opportunities.
   - Analyze your competition. Study existing businesses in your chosen niche to understand what works and what doesn't.
   - Conduct surveys and interviews with potential customers to gather valuable insights into their pain points and preferences.
3. **Solve a Problem:**

- Successful businesses often address a specific problem or pain point. Consider what problems you can solve with your skills, knowledge, or resources.
- Look for inefficiencies or gaps in the current market that your business idea can fill.

4. **Brainstorm Ideas:**
   - Generate a list of potential business ideas. Don't limit yourself at this stage; creativity is key.
   - Consider different business models, such as product-based, service-based, or a combination of both.
   - Collaborate with others to brainstorm ideas and gain diverse perspectives.

5. **Validate Your Idea:**
   - Test the feasibility of your business concept. Create a minimum viable product (MVP) or prototype to see if your idea resonates with potential customers.
   - Seek feedback from friends, family, mentors, or potential customers.
   - Research whether there's a demand for your product or service through online surveys, landing pages, or crowdfunding campaigns.

6. **Consider Your Unique Selling Proposition (USP):**
   - Identify what makes your business idea unique and how it stands out from the competition.
   - Determine the value proposition you offer to customers that will make them choose your product or service.

7. **Create a Business Plan:**
   - Develop a detailed business plan that outlines your idea, target market, marketing strategy, financial projections, and operational plan.
   - A solid business plan is essential for securing funding and guiding your business's growth.

8. **Start Small:**

   - Don't aim for perfection from the beginning. Start small and test your idea in the real market.

- Be prepared to pivot or make adjustments based on customer feedback and market trends.

9. **Seek Support and Mentorship:**
   - Connect with mentors, industry experts, or entrepreneurs who can provide guidance and advice.
   - Join local or online entrepreneurial communities to network and learn from others.

10. **Take Action:**
    - Once you've thoroughly researched, validated, and planned your business idea, take the plunge and start your venture.
    - Be adaptable and open to learning from your experiences.

Remember that finding the right business idea often takes time and persistence. Be willing to iterate and refine your concept as you gain more knowledge and experience in the business world.

1.1 Identifying Your Passion

Identifying your passion is a crucial step in both personal fulfillment and potentially aligning your career or business endeavors with what truly excites and motivates you. Here are some steps to help you identify your passion:

1. **Self-Reflection:**
   - Set aside some quiet time for self-reflection. Think about your past experiences, hobbies, and activities that have brought you joy and fulfillment.
   - Consider the moments when you felt most engaged, enthusiastic, or "in the flow." What were you doing at that time?

2. **Take Note of Your Interests:**
   - Make a list of topics, subjects, or activities that genuinely interest you. These can be broad or specific.
   - Think about what you enjoy reading, watching, or discussing in your free time.

3. **Explore New Activities:**
   - Be open to trying new things. Sometimes, your passion might be something you've never explored before.
   - Join clubs, workshops, or classes related to various interests to discover new passions.

4. **Identify Core Values:**

- Consider your core values and beliefs. What issues or causes are important to you? Your passion may be closely tied to making a positive impact in these areas.

5. **Seek Feedback:**
   - Ask friends, family, and colleagues what they believe you are passionate about. Sometimes, others can provide valuable insights.

6. **Pay Attention to Your Energy Levels:**
   - Notice how different activities make you feel. When you engage in activities aligned with your passion, you often feel energized and motivated rather than drained.

7. **Analyze Your Skills and Strengths:**
   - Think about the skills and strengths you possess. Your passion may be related to activities where you excel or find satisfaction.

8. **Set Goals:**
   - Establish personal and professional goals. Reflect on what you would like to achieve in your life, career, or business.
   - Align your goals with your interests and values to find a path that resonates with you.

9. **Experiment:**
   - It's okay if you don't immediately pinpoint a single passion. Experiment with different activities, projects, or hobbies to test what resonates with you.

10. **Take Your Time:**
    - Identifying your passion is a process that can take time. Be patient with yourself and allow your interests to evolve naturally.

11. **Seek Inspiration:**
    - Read books, watch documentaries, or follow people who are passionate about their pursuits. Their stories can inspire and help you discover your own passion.

12. **Keep a Journal:**
    - Maintain a journal to record your thoughts, experiences, and reflections. Writing can help you clarify your thoughts and identify patterns.

Remember that passions can change and evolve over time, so it's essential to stay open to new experiences and adapt as you discover what truly excites and motivates you. Once you've identified your passion, consider ways to integrate it into your personal and professional life for greater fulfillment and happiness.

1.2 Solving a Problem

Solving a problem is a fundamental aspect of entrepreneurship and innovation. Whether you're starting a business, working on a project, or seeking to improve a process, here are steps to effectively solve a problem:

1. **Identify and Define the Problem:**
   - Clearly articulate the problem you want to solve. Be specific and objective in your description.
   - Analyze the root causes of the problem to understand its underlying factors.
2. **Gather Information and Research:**
   - Collect relevant data, facts, and information related to the problem. This may involve surveys, interviews, market research, or data analysis.
   - Research existing solutions or approaches to see what has been tried before and what worked or didn't work.
3. **Brainstorm Solutions:**
   - Encourage creativity by brainstorming potential solutions. Involve others in the process to gain diverse perspectives.
   - Don't evaluate or judge ideas at this stage; aim for quantity over quality.
4. **Evaluate and Prioritize Solutions:**
   - Assess the feasibility, impact, and cost-effectiveness of each potential solution.
   - Prioritize solutions based on their potential to address the problem effectively.
5. **Develop a Plan:**

   - Create a detailed plan for implementing the chosen solution. Outline the steps, resources, and timeline required.
   - Consider potential risks and challenges and develop mitigation strategies.
6. **Test and Prototype:**

- If applicable, create prototypes or conduct small-scale tests to evaluate the solution's effectiveness before full-scale implementation.
- Use feedback from testing to refine and improve the solution.

7. **Implement the Solution:**
   - Execute the plan and put the solution into action. Ensure that everyone involved understands their roles and responsibilities.
   - Monitor progress and make necessary adjustments as you go along.

8. **Measure and Analyze Results:**
   - Establish key performance indicators (KPIs) to measure the success of the solution.
   - Continuously collect data and analyze results to determine if the problem has been adequately addressed.

9. **Iterate and Improve:**
   - Be open to making further adjustments and refinements to the solution based on ongoing feedback and performance data.
   - Consider the long-term sustainability and scalability of the solution.

10. **Document the Process:**
    - Keep thorough records of the entire problem-solving process, including the problem statement, research, solutions, and outcomes.
    - Documenting the process helps with future reference and learning from past experiences.

11. **Communicate and Collaborate:**
    - Maintain open communication with stakeholders, team members, and any other relevant parties.
    - Collaboration and transparency can lead to better problem-solving outcomes.

12. **Learn from Failures:**
    - Understand that not all solutions will work perfectly. Embrace failures as learning opportunities and adjust your approach accordingly.

13. **Seek Feedback:**
    - Encourage feedback from those affected by the problem and the implemented solution. Their insights can provide valuable input for improvement.

Problem-solving is an ongoing process that requires adaptability and a willingness to learn from your experiences. By following these steps and being persistent, you can develop effective solutions to a wide range of challenges in business and life.

1.3 Identifying Market Gaps

Identifying market gaps is crucial for entrepreneurs and businesses looking to find opportunities for growth and innovation. A market gap represents an unmet need or an area where existing solutions are insufficient. Here's a step-by-step guide on how to identify market gaps:

1. **Understand Market Research:**
   - Start by conducting thorough market research to gain a comprehensive understanding of your industry and target market.
   - Analyze existing data, reports, and studies related to your industry to identify trends, customer preferences, and emerging opportunities.
2. **Define Your Target Audience:**
   - Clearly define your target audience or customer persona. Understand their needs, preferences, pain points, and behaviors.
   - Consider demographic, geographic, psychographic, and behavioral factors that influence your target market.
3. **Competitive Analysis:**
   - Study your competitors to identify gaps in their product or service offerings. Look for areas where they fall short in meeting customer needs.
   - Analyze customer reviews, feedback, and complaints about your competitors' offerings to identify pain points.
4. **Survey and Interview Customers:**
   - Conduct surveys and interviews with potential customers to gather firsthand insights into their needs, challenges, and preferences.
   - Ask open-ended questions to encourage customers to share their unmet needs and areas where they are dissatisfied with current solutions.
5. **Observe Industry Trends:**

- Stay up-to-date with industry news, trends, and innovations. Attend conferences, webinars, and trade shows to learn about emerging technologies and market shifts.
- Look for opportunities to leverage new technologies or approaches to address market gaps.

6. **Analyze Data and Metrics:**
   - Utilize data analytics tools to gather quantitative data about market demand, customer behavior, and competitor performance.
   - Look for patterns and anomalies in the data that might indicate unmet needs or gaps in the market.

7. **Identify Niche Markets:**
   - Explore niche markets within your industry where competition may be lower, and specific needs or preferences are underserved.
   - Niche markets often present opportunities for specialized products or services.

8. **Stay Customer-Centric:**
   - Always keep the customer at the center of your analysis. Ensure that any identified market gap aligns with real customer needs and pain points.

9. **SWOT Analysis:**
   - Conduct a SWOT (Strengths, Weaknesses, Opportunities, Threats) analysis to assess your business's strengths and weaknesses in addressing market gaps.
   - Use this analysis to identify strategic opportunities for growth.

10. Innovation and Creativity:
    - Encourage innovation within your organization. Brainstorm new product or service ideas that could fill identified market gaps.
    - Consider how you can improve upon existing solutions to provide more value to customers.

11. **Market Validation:**
    - Before fully committing resources, validate your findings by conducting small-scale tests, surveys, or pilot projects.
    - Ensure that there is genuine demand for your proposed solution.

12. **Business Plan Development:**

- Once you've identified a viable market gap, create a comprehensive business plan that outlines your strategy, target market, marketing plan, and financial projections.

13. Launch and Iterate:
- Launch your product or service and be prepared to iterate and refine your offerings based on customer feedback and market dynamics.

Identifying market gaps requires ongoing vigilance and adaptability. Markets evolve, and customer needs change, so it's essential to stay attuned to these shifts and adjust your strategies accordingly. When you successfully identify and address market gaps, you can gain a competitive edge and provide valuable solutions to customers.

1.4 Analyzing Trends

Analyzing trends is a crucial activity for individuals, businesses, and organizations in various fields, from marketing and finance to technology and fashion. Here's a step-by-step guide on how to effectively analyze trends:

1. **Define Your Area of Interest:**
   - Start by clearly defining the area or industry you want to analyze for trends. This could be related to your business, a specific market, or a personal interest.
2. **Gather Data and Information:**
   - Collect data from reputable sources such as industry reports, government agencies, market research firms, and academic studies.
   - Utilize online resources, databases, and news sources to stay up-to-date with current events and developments in your chosen area.
3. **Set Up Alerts:**
   - Use online tools and services to set up alerts or notifications for keywords and topics related to your area of interest. This will help you receive real-time updates on relevant news and trends.
4. **Analyze Historical Data:**
   - Review historical data and trends to identify patterns and changes over time. This provides context for understanding current trends.

- Consider using data visualization tools to make complex trends more accessible and easier to understand.

5. **Identify Key Indicators:**
   - Determine which key performance indicators (KPIs) or metrics are most relevant to your analysis. For example, in finance, this might include stock prices, while in marketing, it could be website traffic or social media engagement.

6. **Look for Patterns and Anomalies:**
   - Analyze the data to identify recurring patterns, correlations, or anomalies. Trends often emerge from significant data points or shifts in the status quo.

7. **Consider External Factors:**
   - Recognize that trends can be influenced by external factors such as economic conditions, technological advancements, regulatory changes, or cultural shifts.
   - Analyze how these external factors might impact the trends you're observing.

8. **Segment Your Data:**
   - Segment your data by different variables, such as demographics, geography, or product categories. This can reveal more nuanced trends within your chosen area.

9. **Conduct Surveys and Interviews:**
   - If applicable, conduct surveys and interviews with relevant stakeholders, customers, or experts to gather qualitative insights and opinions on emerging trends.

10. **Competitor Analysis:**
    - Study your competitors and their strategies. Analyze their products, services, marketing approaches, and customer feedback to identify trends they are capitalizing on.

11. **Stay Informed Through Networking:**
    - Attend industry conferences, webinars, and networking events to connect with professionals who can provide valuable insights into current trends.

12. **Scenario Planning:**
    - Consider different scenarios and potential future developments based on the trends you've identified. This can help with strategic planning and risk assessment.

13. **Evaluate Impact and Opportunities:**

- Assess the impact of identified trends on your business, industry, or area of interest. Determine whether they present opportunities or threats.

14. Create an Action Plan:
- Based on your analysis, develop an action plan that outlines how you or your organization can respond to the trends. This might include adjusting strategies, investing in new technologies, or entering new markets.

15. Monitor and Adapt:
- Continuously monitor the trends you've identified. Trends evolve, and it's essential to adapt your strategies accordingly to stay competitive and relevant.

16. Share Findings:
- If you're analyzing trends within an organization, share your findings with relevant stakeholders to ensure everyone is informed and aligned with potential actions.

Effective trend analysis requires a combination of data-driven insights, qualitative research, and a keen understanding of the specific industry or area you're examining. By staying vigilant and proactive, you can position yourself or your organization to capitalize on emerging opportunities and navigate challenges effectively.

M arket research and validation are essential steps in the process of developing and launching a product or service. These processes help you gather information, assess market demand, and ensure that your business idea has the potential to succeed. Here's an overview of market research and validation:

1. Market Research:

Market research involves collecting and analyzing information about your target market, industry, and competition. The goal is to understand the market landscape and identify opportunities and challenges. Here are some key aspects of market research:

   a. **Target Audience:** Define your ideal customer persona. Understand their demographics, preferences, pain points, and behavior.
   b. **Industry Analysis:** Study the overall industry in which you plan to operate. Identify trends, growth rates, and potential disruptions.
   c. **Competitive Analysis:** Analyze your competitors, their strengths, weaknesses, and market positioning. Determine what sets your offering apart.

d. **Market Size and Growth:** Estimate the size of your target market and its growth potential. This helps you assess the revenue potential.
e. **Customer Surveys and Interviews:** Gather direct feedback from potential customers through surveys and interviews. Understand their needs, preferences, and pain points.
f. **Secondary Research:** Use existing data, reports, and studies to gather information about the market. This can include government data, industry publications, and academic research.

2. **Market Validation:**

Market validation goes beyond research; it involves taking steps to test your business idea and gather real-world evidence of demand. Here are some strategies for market validation:

a. **Minimum Viable Product (MVP):** Create a simplified version of your product or service and launch it to a small group of early adopters. Collect feedback and iterate based on their responses.
b. **Crowdfunding:** Use platforms like Kickstarter or Indiegogo to gauge interest and raise initial funding. Successful crowdfunding campaigns can be a strong validation of your idea.
c. **Pilot Programs:** Partner with a small number of customers or businesses to test your offering in a controlled environment. Gather feedback and refine your offering before a full-scale launch.
d. **A/B Testing:** If you have a digital product or service, conduct A/B tests to compare different features or marketing approaches to see which resonates best with your target audience.
e. **Sales and Pre-orders:** Offer your product or service for sale or pre-order and measure the actual demand. Be transparent about delivery timelines to manage customer expectations.
f. **Landing Pages:** Create landing pages or websites to promote your offering and capture email addresses of interested prospects. The number of sign-ups can indicate interest.
g. **Focus Groups:** Organize focus groups with potential customers to get their reactions and insights about your product or service.
h. **Iterate and Pivot:** Based on the feedback and data collected during market validation, be prepared to make changes to your product, pricing, or marketing strategy. Sometimes, this may

involve pivoting to a different target market or adjusting your offering.

Market research and validation are ongoing processes that continue even after you've launched your product or service. Continuously gathering feedback, monitoring market trends, and adapting to changes are crucial for long-term success in business.

2.1 Understanding Your Target Audience

Understanding your target audience is a fundamental step in developing a successful product, service, or marketing strategy. When you have a deep understanding of your target audience, you can tailor your offerings to meet their specific needs and preferences. Here's how to go about understanding your target audience:

1. **Demographics:**

Start by gathering information about the basic characteristics of your target audience. This includes factors such as:

- Age
- Gender
- Location
- Income level
- Education level
- Occupation
- Demographic data helps you create a general profile of your audience.

2. **Psychographics:**

Psychographics delve deeper into the psychological and lifestyle aspects of your audience. Consider:

- Interests and hobbies
- Values and beliefs
- Attitudes
- Lifestyle choices
- Pain points and challenges
- Understanding psychographics helps you connect with your audience on a more emotional level.

3. **Behavioral Insights:**

Analyze the behavior of your target audience, both online and offline. This includes:

- Online behavior: Websites they visit, social media platforms they use, content they engage with, and online shopping habits.
- Offline behavior: Shopping habits, leisure activities, and preferred communication channels.
- Behavioral insights help you determine where and how to reach your audience effectively.

4. **Needs and Pain Points:**
   - Identify the specific needs, problems, and pain points that your target audience faces. This information is critical for crafting solutions that address their challenges.

5. **Market Research:**
   - Conduct market research to gather data on market trends, competitor offerings, and customer preferences. This research can be quantitative (surveys, data analysis) or qualitative (interviews, focus groups).

6. **Customer Surveys and Interviews:**
   - Directly engage with members of your target audience through surveys and interviews. Ask questions about their preferences, opinions, and experiences related to your industry or niche.

7. **Create Buyer Personas:**
   - Based on the data you've collected, create detailed buyer personas. These are fictional representations of your ideal customers, including their demographics, psychographics, pain points, and goals. Having buyer personas makes it easier to align your strategies with the needs of different segments within your target audience.

8. **Test and Iterate:**
   - Implement strategies, products, or services based on your understanding of your target audience. Be prepared to test different approaches and iterate based on the feedback and results you receive.

9. **Competitive Analysis:**
   - Analyze your competitors to understand how they are catering to the same or similar target audiences. Identify gaps or opportunities where you can differentiate yourself.

10. **Feedback Loop:**

- Maintain an ongoing feedback loop with your audience. Listen to their feedback, whether it's through customer support interactions, surveys, or social media. Use this feedback to continuously improve your offerings.

11. Monitor Trends:
- Stay updated on industry trends and changes in consumer behavior. Adapt your strategies accordingly to remain relevant to your target audience.

Remember that your target audience may evolve over time, so it's essential to stay flexible and adjust your approach as needed. Regularly revisit your audience research to ensure you're meeting their current needs and preferences.

2.2 Competitor Analysis

Competitor analysis is a crucial component of any business strategy. By understanding your competitors, you can identify opportunities, threats, and areas for differentiation. Here's how to conduct a comprehensive competitor analysis:

1. **Identify Your Competitors:**
   - Start by identifying who your direct and indirect competitors are. Direct competitors offer similar products or services to the same target audience, while indirect competitors may serve a slightly different need but still compete for your audience's attention and budget.

2. **Gather Information:**

Collect data and information about your competitors. This can include:

- **Products or Services:** What do they offer, and how do their offerings compare to yours in terms of features, quality, and pricing?
- **Market Share:** Do they dominate a particular segment of the market?
- **Pricing Strategy:** What are their pricing models, and how do they position themselves in terms of value?
- **Distribution Channels:** How do they reach customers (e.g., online, retail, partnerships)?
- **Marketing and Branding:** Analyze their marketing campaigns, branding strategies, and messaging.

- **Customer Reviews and Feedback:** Read customer reviews, social media comments, and feedback to understand what customers like and dislike about their offerings.
- **Financial Performance:** If possible, gather financial data such as revenue, profitability, and growth rates.
- **SWOT Analysis:** Conduct a SWOT analysis for each competitor, outlining their strengths, weaknesses, opportunities, and threats.

3. **Competitive Positioning:**
   - Determine where you stand in relation to your competitors. Are you offering something unique or superior? Are you competing on price, quality, innovation, or some other factor? Understanding your competitive positioning helps you identify areas where you can excel.

4. **Market Share and Market Trends:**
   - Analyze market share data to see how your competitors are performing in the market. Are they gaining or losing market share? Additionally, monitor market trends and changes in consumer behavior to stay ahead of the competition.

5. **Customer Insights:**
   - Gather information about your competitors' customer base. This may involve understanding their demographics, psychographics, and buying behavior. You can also use surveys, focus groups, or social media monitoring to gain insights into their customers' preferences and pain points.

6. **Differentiation Opportunities:**
   - Identify opportunities to differentiate your business from competitors. This could involve offering unique features, improving customer service, or adopting a pricing strategy that sets you apart.

7. **SWOT Analysis for Your Business:**
   - Conduct a SWOT analysis for your own business, comparing it to your competitors. This can help you identify areas where you need to improve and where you have a competitive advantage.

8. **Competitive Benchmarking:**
   - Benchmark your performance against key competitors in areas such as customer satisfaction, product quality, delivery times, and pricing. Use this information to set performance goals.

9. **Track Changes and Evolve:**

- Competitor analysis should be an ongoing process. Continuously monitor your competitors and adapt your strategies as the competitive landscape evolves.

10. Legal and Ethical Considerations:
- Be mindful of legal and ethical boundaries when conducting competitor analysis. Avoid illegal or unethical practices such as corporate espionage or spreading false information about competitors.

Remember that the goal of competitor analysis is not just to copy what your competitors are doing but to gain insights that inform your own strategic decisions. Use this information to refine your business strategy, improve your offerings, and better meet the needs of your target audience.

2.3 Minimum Viable Product (MVP)

A Minimum Viable Product (MVP) is a concept from the field of product development and startup management. It represents a stripped-down version of a product that includes only the essential features and functionality needed to satisfy early adopters and gather feedback for further development. The primary goal of an MVP is to quickly validate or invalidate key assumptions about a product or service with minimal resources invested. Here are the key components and principles of an MVP:

1. **Essential Features:** An MVP includes only the core features that address the primary problem or need your product is intended to solve. These features should be enough to deliver value to early users.
2. **Rapid Development:** The development of an MVP should be fast and cost-effective. The emphasis is on getting a functional version of the product to market as quickly as possible to test its viability.
3. **User-Centric:** The focus of an MVP is on user feedback and validation. It's critical to target a specific group of early adopters who are willing to use the product and provide feedback.
4. **Feedback Collection:** The MVP is a tool for gathering feedback and data from real users. This feedback helps you understand whether your product meets users' needs and what improvements are necessary.

5. **Iterative Process:** Based on the feedback received, you iterate on the MVP to make improvements and enhancements. This iterative approach allows you to refine the product gradually.
6. **Risk Reduction:** An MVP helps mitigate risks associated with developing a full-fledged product that might not find a market fit. By testing your assumptions early, you can make informed decisions about whether to invest further.
7. **Lean Approach:** The MVP concept is closely associated with the lean startup methodology, which encourages efficient resource allocation and a focus on validated learning.
8. **Market Testing:** An MVP can be used to test the market and gauge interest in your product before committing significant resources to a full launch.
9. **Cost Efficiency:** Building an MVP typically costs less than developing a complete product. This allows startups and businesses to conserve resources while still making progress.

Examples of MVPs can vary widely based on the product or service being developed. For a software application, an MVP might be a basic version with a limited set of features. For a physical product, it could be a prototype with the core functionality. The specifics depend on the nature of the business and its goals.

Once you've gathered enough feedback and data through your MVP, you can make informed decisions about whether to pivot (change your product direction), persevere (continue refining and expanding the product), or abandon the project altogether. MVPs are a valuable tool for reducing uncertainty and increasing the chances of success in product development and entrepreneurship.

2.4 Gathering Feedback
Gathering feedback is a crucial part of improving products, services, processes, and overall business operations. It helps you understand what's working well and what needs improvement, whether you're running a business, developing a product, or managing a team. Here are some effective ways to gather feedback:

1. **Surveys:**

- **Online Surveys:** Create online surveys using tools like Google Forms, SurveyMonkey, or Typeform. Send these surveys to your target audience via email, social media, or your website.
- **In-Person Surveys:** Conduct face-to-face surveys at events, conferences, or physical locations where your audience gathers.
- **Phone Surveys:** Reach out to customers or stakeholders via phone and ask structured questions to gather feedback.

2. **Feedback Forms:**
   - **Website Feedback Forms:** Place feedback forms on your website or within your product/service to collect input directly from users.
   - **Customer Service Forms:** Include feedback sections in your customer support interactions to gather insights on customer experiences.

3. **Interviews:**
   - Conduct one-on-one interviews with customers, clients, or team members to have in-depth conversations about their experiences, needs, and suggestions.
   - **Focus Group Interviews:** Gather small groups of people to discuss specific topics or products. This can be especially useful for testing new ideas or concepts.

4. **Social Media Listening:**
   - Monitor social media platforms for mentions, comments, and discussions related to your brand, products, or industry. Respond to comments and engage in conversations.
   - Use social media listening tools to track and analyze mentions and sentiment.

5. **Online Reviews and Ratings:**
   - Pay attention to online reviews on platforms like Google Reviews, Yelp, Amazon, or industry-specific review sites.
   - Encourage customers to leave reviews by providing excellent service and requesting feedback after transactions.

6. **Customer Feedback Tools:**
   - Implement customer feedback tools like Net Promoter Score (NPS) surveys, Customer Satisfaction (CSAT) surveys, or Customer Effort Score (CES) surveys to measure specific aspects of customer satisfaction.

- Use feedback management software to collect, analyze, and organize feedback data.
7. **Feedback Widgets and Buttons:**
   - Add feedback widgets or buttons to your website or app, making it easy for users to share their thoughts or report issues.
8. **Email Feedback Requests:**
   - Send targeted email requests for feedback to your customer database. Make it easy for recipients to provide input by including clickable links or buttons.
9. **Employee Surveys:**
   - Gather feedback from employees through regular surveys to assess workplace satisfaction, identify areas for improvement, and uncover ideas for innovation.
10. **Observation and User Testing:**
    - Observe users interacting with your product or service in real-life situations or through usability testing to identify usability issues and user preferences.
11. **Feedback Kiosks:**
    - Implement feedback kiosks in physical locations such as retail stores, restaurants, or public spaces to gather on-site feedback from customers.
12. **Anonymous Feedback:**
    - Allow users or employees to provide feedback anonymously, which can encourage more honest and candid responses.
13. **Feedback Hotlines:**
    - Establish feedback hotlines or dedicated phone numbers for users or customers to call and share their thoughts or report issues.
14. **Third-Party Surveys and Audits:**
    - Hire external firms or consultants to conduct surveys, audits, or assessments to gain an unbiased perspective.
15. **Feedback through Social Media Polls and Questions:**
    - Use social media platforms to run polls or ask questions to engage your audience and gather insights on specific topics or preferences.
16. **Collaborative Tools:**

- Use collaborative tools like Slack, Microsoft Teams, or project management software to create feedback channels where team members can share ideas and suggestions.

Remember that collecting feedback is just the first step. To make it truly valuable, you should analyze the feedback, identify common themes or patterns, prioritize action items, and take steps to address the issues or implement suggested improvements. Regularly soliciting and acting on feedback can lead to better products, improved customer satisfaction, and more efficient business operations.

C reating a business plan is a critical step when starting a new business or seeking funding for an existing one. A well-structured business plan outlines your business goals, strategies, and financial projections, serving as a roadmap for your venture's success. Here are the key components to include in your business plan:

1. **Executive Summary:**
   - Provide a concise overview of your business, its mission, and its unique value proposition.
   - Summarize the key points from each section of your plan.
2. **Business Description:**
   - Describe your business concept, its history, and its legal structure (e.g., sole proprietorship, LLC, corporation).
   - Explain your business's purpose and how it addresses a specific market need.
3. **Market Analysis:**
   - Research your target market, including its size, demographics, and buying behavior.
   - Analyze your competitors and identify your competitive advantage.
   - Highlight market trends and growth potential.
4. **Organization and Management:**

- Introduce your management team, including their qualifications and roles.
- Outline your organizational structure and any partnerships or key suppliers.

5. **Product or Service Line:**
   - Describe your products or services in detail.
   - Explain their features, benefits, and unique selling points.
   - Discuss any intellectual property or proprietary technology.

6. **Sales and Marketing Strategy:**
   - Outline your marketing plan, including your target audience, pricing strategy, and distribution channels.
   - Define your sales strategy, including your sales team, sales process, and sales forecast.

7. **Funding Request (if applicable):**
   - Specify the amount of funding you need and how you'll use it.
   - Provide details about the type of funding you're seeking (e.g., equity investment, loans).

8. **Financial Projections:**
   - Include projected income statements, balance sheets, and cash flow statements for at least the next three to five years.
   - Highlight assumptions and explain how you arrived at your financial forecasts.
   - Conduct a break-even analysis.

9. **Appendix (optional):**
   - Include any additional information that supports your business plan, such as resumes of key team members, market research data, or product/service images.

10. **Exit Strategy (if applicable):**
    - Discuss your long-term plans for the business, whether it's to sell, go public, or continue as a sustainable enterprise.

11. **Tips for creating a successful business plan:**
    - Be concise and clear. Avoid jargon and unnecessary technical language.
    - Tailor your plan to your audience (e.g., investors, lenders, internal use).
    - Keep it realistic. Don't overinflate financial projections or make unrealistic claims.
    - Update your business plan regularly as your business evolves.

- Seek feedback from mentors, advisors, or industry experts.
- Be prepared to defend and discuss the contents of your plan in detail during presentations or meetings.

Remember that a well-thought-out business plan not only serves as a roadmap for your business but also demonstrates your commitment and professionalism to potential stakeholders.

3.1 Financial Projections

Financial projections are a critical component of your business plan and provide a detailed look at how your business is expected to perform financially in the future. These projections help potential investors, lenders, and stakeholders understand the economic viability and growth potential of your business. Here's how to create financial projections:

1. **Income Statement (Profit and Loss Statement):**

This statement summarizes your revenue, expenses, and profits over a specific period, typically monthly or annually. It includes:

- **Sales or revenue:** Estimate your sales based on market research, pricing, and sales forecasts.
- **Cost of goods sold (COGS):** Calculate the direct costs associated with producing your product or delivering your service.
- **Gross profit:** Subtract COGS from revenue.
- **Operating expenses:** Include all expenses such as rent, utilities, salaries, marketing costs, and administrative expenses.
- **Operating profit (or EBIT):** Subtract operating expenses from gross profit.
- **Interest and taxes:** Account for interest expenses and taxes, if applicable.
- **Net profit (or net income):** Subtract interest and taxes from operating profit.

2. **Balance Sheet:**

The balance sheet provides a snapshot of your business's financial position at a specific point in time. It includes:

- **Assets:** List your current assets (e.g., cash, accounts receivable, inventory) and non-current assets (e.g., property, equipment).

- **Liabilities:** Detail your current liabilities (e.g., accounts payable, short-term loans) and long-term liabilities (e.g., long-term loans, mortgages).
- **Equity:** Calculate your owner's equity by subtracting total liabilities from total assets.

3. **Cash Flow Statement:**

This statement tracks the cash inflows and outflows of your business. It includes:

- **Operating activities:** Detail cash generated or spent in your day-to-day operations.
- **Investing activities:** Record cash used for or generated from investments in assets like equipment or acquisitions.
- **Financing activities:** Track cash flows related to loans, equity investments, or dividend payments.

4. **Sales Forecast:**
   - Provide a detailed breakdown of your expected sales by product or service category and by month or quarter.
   - Consider historical sales data, market research, and seasonality in your projections.

5. **Expense Projections:**
   - Estimate your operating expenses, such as rent, utilities, marketing, and payroll, on a monthly or annual basis.
   - Be sure to account for any anticipated increases in expenses as your business grows.

6. **Break-Even Analysis:**
   - Calculate the point at which your total revenue equals your total expenses, resulting in zero profit or loss.
   - This analysis helps determine how many units or sales are needed to cover costs.

7. **Assumptions and Justifications:**
   - Clearly outline the assumptions behind your financial projections, such as growth rates, pricing strategies, and market conditions.
   - Explain the reasoning and data supporting these assumptions.

8. **Sensitivity Analysis:**

- Conduct sensitivity analysis to assess how changes in key variables (e.g., sales volume, pricing, expenses) would impact your financial results.

9. **Financial Ratios (optional):**
   - Include relevant financial ratios, such as liquidity, profitability, and debt ratios, to provide a deeper understanding of your business's financial health.

10. **Footnotes and Explanations:**
    - Add any necessary footnotes and explanations to clarify complex financial data or unusual items.

It's essential to update your financial projections regularly to reflect actual performance and adjust your business strategies accordingly. Also, seek the input of financial experts or advisors to ensure your projections are realistic and credible. Sound financial projections are crucial for making informed business decisions and securing financing from investors or lenders.

3.2 Operations Plan

An operations plan is a crucial component of your business plan that outlines how your business will function on a day-to-day basis. It provides a detailed roadmap for executing your business strategy, managing resources, and delivering products or services efficiently. Here's how to create an effective operations plan:

1. **Business Location and Facilities:**
   - Describe the physical location of your business, including details about the property, lease agreements, and any necessary permits or licenses.
   - Explain how the location supports your business operations.

2. **Production Process (if applicable):**
   - If you are involved in manufacturing or production, detail the steps involved in your production process.
   - Discuss the equipment, technology, and materials required for production.

3. **Supply Chain Management:**
   - Explain how you will source raw materials, components, or products if applicable.
   - Detail your relationships with suppliers and any backup plans for supply chain disruptions.

4. **Inventory Management:**
   - Outline your inventory control methods, including how you will track, order, and manage inventory levels.
   - Discuss strategies for minimizing excess inventory and carrying costs.
5. **Quality Control and Assurance:**
   - Describe your quality control processes to ensure that your products or services meet or exceed customer expectations.
   - Detail any quality assurance certifications or standards your business adheres to.
6. **Production Capacity and Scalability:**
   - Discuss your current production capacity and how you plan to scale it as your business grows.
   - Highlight any bottlenecks or constraints in your production process and how you plan to address them.
7. **Technology and Information Systems:**
   - Explain the role of technology and information systems in your operations, such as inventory management software, point-of-sale systems, or customer relationship management (CRM) tools.
   - Describe any plans for technology upgrades or improvements.
8. **Staffing and Human Resources:**
   - Detail your staffing requirements, including the number of employees, their roles, and qualifications.
   - Explain your hiring and training processes.
   - Discuss your workforce management strategies, including employee retention and performance evaluation.
9. **Legal and Regulatory Compliance:**
   - Describe how your business will comply with relevant laws, regulations, and industry standards.
   - Explain any permits or licenses required for your operations.
10. **Health and Safety Protocols:**
    - Outline safety procedures and protocols to ensure the well-being of employees, customers, and visitors.
    - Explain how you will handle emergencies or unforeseen incidents.
11. **Customer Service and Support:**

- Detail your customer service policies and procedures, including response times and methods of communication.
- Explain how you will handle customer inquiries, complaints, and feedback.

12. Supplier Relationships:
- Discuss your relationships with key suppliers and vendors, including payment terms and agreements.
- Describe any strategies for optimizing supplier relationships.

13. Environmental Sustainability (if applicable):
- Explain any environmentally friendly practices or initiatives your business is implementing.
- Detail how you plan to minimize your environmental impact.

14. Risk Management:
- Identify potential risks to your operations and strategies to mitigate them.
- Include contingency plans for handling unexpected challenges.

15. Timeline and Milestones:
- Create a timeline that outlines key operational milestones and their projected completion dates.
- This can help you track progress and stay on schedule.

Your operations plan should align with your overall business strategy and goals, demonstrating how you intend to efficiently deliver value to your customers while managing resources effectively. It's important to regularly review and update your operations plan as your business evolves and grows to ensure its continued relevance and effectiveness.

3.3 Funding and Investment

Securing funding and investment is a critical step for many businesses, whether you're starting a new venture or looking to expand an existing one. Here's a guide on how to approach funding and investment for your business:

1. Determine Funding Needs:
- Calculate how much capital you need for your business. Consider startup costs, operational expenses, and growth plans.
- Be specific about how you'll use the funds. Investors want to know their money will be put to good use.

2. Bootstrap if Possible:

- Consider funding your business through personal savings, revenue generated by the business, or loans from friends and family before seeking external investment.
- Bootstrapping can help you retain full control of your business and reduce the need for outside investors.

3. **Types of Funding:**

Explore different sources of funding, such as:

- **Equity Financing:** Involves selling ownership shares in your company to investors in exchange for capital. Common options include angel investors and venture capitalists.
- **Debt Financing:** Involves borrowing money that you'll need to repay with interest. Sources include bank loans, online lenders, and business credit cards.
- **Crowdfunding:** Raise capital from a large number of people through platforms like Kickstarter, Indiegogo, or equity crowdfunding platforms.
- **Grants and Competitions:** Look for grants, awards, or startup competitions that align with your business idea. These often don't require equity or repayment.
- **Self-Financing:** Use personal savings, assets, or income generated by the business to fund your startup.

4. **Develop a Business Plan:**
- A well-documented business plan is crucial when seeking funding. It demonstrates your commitment and the potential return on investment.
- Tailor your plan to the specific needs and expectations of potential investors.

5. **Identify the Right Investors:**
- Research and target investors or funding sources that align with your business's industry, stage, and goals.
- Network and attend industry events to connect with potential investors.

6. **Pitch Your Business:**
- Prepare a compelling pitch that highlights your business's unique value proposition, market opportunity, financial projections, and team.

- Customize your pitch to the preferences and criteria of different investors.

7. **Due Diligence:**
   - Expect potential investors to conduct due diligence on your business. Be prepared to provide detailed financial records, contracts, and other relevant documents.
   - Be transparent and honest throughout the due diligence process.

8. **Negotiate Terms:**
   - When you receive offers from investors, carefully review the terms and negotiate if necessary. Pay attention to valuation, equity stake, and control.
   - Consult with legal and financial advisors to ensure you fully understand the terms and implications.

9. **Legal and Regulatory Compliance:**
   - Comply with all legal and regulatory requirements related to raising capital, especially when dealing with securities laws.
   - Consult legal experts to ensure you are in compliance.

10. **Documentation and Agreements:**
    - Create comprehensive investment agreements that outline the terms and conditions of the investment, including rights, responsibilities, and exit strategies.

11. **Maintain Open Communication:**
    - Keep investors informed about your business's progress and challenges. Regular updates build trust and confidence.

12. **Use Funds Wisely:**
    - Ensure that the funds are used as outlined in your business plan. Mismanagement of funds can lead to investor dissatisfaction.

13. **Plan for an Exit Strategy:**
    - Consider how you or your investors will eventually exit the business, whether through acquisition, IPO, or other means. Share this plan with investors.

14. **Seek Professional Advice:**
    - Consult with lawyers, accountants, financial advisors, and business consultants as needed to navigate the complexities of funding and investment.

Remember that securing funding can be a lengthy process, and rejection is common. It's essential to be persistent and refine your pitch and business plan based on feedback and market dynamics. Additionally, always seek legal and financial advice when dealing with investment transactions to protect your interests and those of your investors.

L egal and regulatory considerations are essential aspects of any business or organization's operations. They encompass a wide range of laws, rules, and regulations that govern various aspects of business activities. Failing to comply with these legal and regulatory requirements can lead to legal liabilities, fines, and reputational damage. Here are some key legal and regulatory considerations for businesses:

1. **Business Structure and Registration:**
   - Choose the appropriate legal structure for your business (e.g., sole proprietorship, partnership, LLC, corporation) and register it with the relevant authorities.
   - Comply with local, state, and federal registration and licensing requirements.
2. **Taxation:**
   - Understand and comply with tax laws and regulations, including income tax, sales tax, and payroll tax.
   - Keep accurate financial records and file tax returns on time.
3. **Employment and Labor Laws:**
   - Adhere to employment laws related to hiring, termination, discrimination, wage and hour regulations, and workplace safety.

- Comply with labor laws such as the Fair Labor Standards Act (FLSA) and the Family and Medical Leave Act (FMLA).

4. **Intellectual Property:**
   - Protect your intellectual property through patents, trademarks, and copyrights.
   - Avoid infringing on the intellectual property rights of others.

5. **Contractual Agreements:**
   - Draft and execute contracts carefully, and ensure they are legally enforceable.
   - Understand the terms and conditions of contracts with customers, suppliers, and partners.

6. **Data Privacy and Security:**
   - Comply with data protection laws (e.g., GDPR, CCPA) if you collect and store customer or employee data.
   - Implement security measures to safeguard sensitive information.

7. **Environmental Regulations:**
   - Comply with environmental laws and regulations relevant to your industry.
   - Take measures to minimize your environmental footprint.

8. **Antitrust and Competition Laws:**
   - Avoid engaging in anticompetitive practices, such as price-fixing or monopolistic behavior.
   - Understand and adhere to antitrust laws and regulations.

9. **Consumer Protection:**
   - Ensure your business practices and marketing are in line with consumer protection laws.
   - Be transparent and honest in advertising and product labeling.

10. **Health and Safety Regulations:**
    - Implement workplace safety measures to protect employees and customers.
    - Comply with industry-specific health and safety regulations.

11. **International Trade and Export Control:**
    - If applicable, adhere to international trade laws, export controls, and sanctions.
    - Ensure compliance with customs and import/export regulations.

12. **Financial Regulations:**

- Comply with financial regulations if your business involves banking, securities, or financial services.
- Maintain accurate financial records and report as required.

13. Ethical and Corporate Responsibility:
- Consider ethical standards and corporate responsibility in your business practices.
- Avoid engaging in unethical behavior that could harm your reputation.

14. Litigation and Dispute Resolution:
- Be prepared to handle legal disputes through negotiation, mediation, arbitration, or litigation if necessary.

15. Government Regulations and Industry-specific Compliance:
- Stay informed about industry-specific regulations and government policies that affect your business.

To navigate these legal and regulatory considerations effectively, it's advisable to consult with legal professionals, such as attorneys and regulatory experts, who can provide guidance and ensure compliance with the applicable laws and regulations in your jurisdiction and industry. Regularly reviewing and updating your compliance procedures is also crucial to adapt to changing legal landscapes.

4.1 Choosing a Business Structure

Choosing the right business structure is a critical decision when starting a business. The business structure you select will affect various aspects of your company, including taxation, liability, management, and funding options. Here are some common business structures and factors to consider when choosing one:

1. Sole Proprietorship:
- **Ownership:** You are the sole owner and have full control over the business.
- **Liability:** You have unlimited personal liability for business debts and obligations.
- **Taxation:** Business income is reported on your personal tax return (Schedule C).
- **Ease of Setup:** It's relatively simple and inexpensive to establish.
- **Management:** You have full control but may have limited capacity for growth.

- **Funding:** Typically relies on personal savings and loans.

2. **Partnership:**
   - **Ownership:** Owned and operated by two or more individuals or entities.
   - **Liability:** Partners have shared liability for business debts and obligations.
   - **Taxation:** Business income passes through to partners' personal tax returns.
   - **Ease of Setup:** Requires a partnership agreement and registration in some cases.
   - **Management:** Partners share control and decision-making.
   - **Funding:** Partners contribute capital and may seek additional funding.

3. **Limited Liability Company (LLC):**
   - **Ownership:** Owners are called members; can be individuals or entities.
   - **Liability:** Members' personal assets are protected from business debts and liabilities.
   - **Taxation:** Flexibility to choose between pass-through taxation (like a partnership) or corporate taxation.
   - **Ease of Setup:** Requires articles of organization and an operating agreement.
   - **Management:** Can be member-managed or manager-managed.
   - **Funding:** Members contribute capital; can attract outside investors.

4. **Corporation (C-Corp or S-Corp):**
   - **Ownership:** Owned by shareholders, with a board of directors and officers managing the company.
   - **Liability:** Shareholders have limited liability; personal assets are generally protected.
   - **Taxation:** C-Corps face double taxation (corporate and individual), while S-Corps have pass-through taxation.
   - **Ease of Setup:** Requires articles of incorporation, bylaws, and regular corporate compliance.
   - **Management:** Shareholders elect a board of directors, which appoints officers.
   - **Funding:** Easier access to capital through stock sales.

5. **Nonprofit Organization:**

- **Ownership:** Governed by a board of directors or trustees.
- **Liability:** Limited liability for members and directors.
- **Taxation:** Typically tax-exempt at the federal and state levels, but must comply with nonprofit regulations.
- **Ease of Setup:** Requires incorporation and adherence to nonprofit laws.
- **Management:** Managed by a board of directors or trustees.
- **Funding:** Relies on donations, grants, and fundraising efforts.

When choosing a business structure, consider factors such as your business's size, industry, growth potential, and your personal preferences regarding control and liability. It's essential to consult with legal and financial professionals to understand the legal and tax implications fully. Additionally, the specific rules and requirements for business structures can vary by jurisdiction, so it's essential to research and comply with local regulations.

4.2 Registering Your Business

Registering your business is a crucial step in the process of starting and legalizing your company. The requirements for business registration can vary significantly depending on your location, business structure, and industry. Here are the general steps and considerations for registering your business:

1. **Choose a Business Name:**
    - Select a unique and suitable name for your business. Ensure it complies with naming rules and regulations in your jurisdiction.
2. **Determine Your Business Structure:**
    - Decide on the legal structure of your business (e.g., sole proprietorship, partnership, LLC, corporation). This will impact your registration process.
3. **Register with the Appropriate Authorities:**
    - Register your business with the relevant government authorities. The specific agency will depend on your location and business structure.
    - **Sole Proprietorship/Partnership:** You may need to register your business name (also known as a "Doing Business As" or DBA name) with the local county or city clerk's office. Check with your local government for specific requirements.

- **Limited Liability Company (LLC):** File articles of organization with the state's secretary of state or equivalent agency. You may also need an operating agreement.
- **Corporation (C-Corp or S-Corp):** File articles of incorporation with the state's secretary of state or equivalent agency. You'll also need corporate bylaws.

4. **Obtain an Employer Identification Number (EIN):**
   - An EIN, also known as a federal tax identification number, is required for most businesses. You can obtain one from the Internal Revenue Service (IRS) either online or by submitting Form SS-4.

5. **Register for State and Local Taxes:**
   - Depending on your location and business type, you may need to register for state sales tax, use tax, and other state and local taxes. Check with your state's Department of Revenue or Taxation for guidance.

6. **Business Licenses and Permits:**
   - Determine what licenses and permits are required for your specific industry and location. This can include health permits, professional licenses, and more.

7. **Regulatory Compliance:**
   - If your business operates in a regulated industry (e.g., healthcare, finance, food service), you may need to comply with specific industry regulations and licensing requirements.

8. **Zoning and Land Use Compliance:**
   - Ensure that your business location complies with zoning and land use regulations in your area. Some businesses may require special zoning permits.

9. **Intellectual Property Protection:**
   - If applicable, consider registering trademarks or patents to protect your intellectual property.

10. **Insurance:**
   - Explore business insurance options, including general liability insurance, workers' compensation, and any industry-specific coverage you may need.

11. **Local Business Associations:**

- Consider joining local business associations or chambers of commerce. They can provide networking opportunities and resources for new businesses.

12. **Compliance with Federal Regulations:**
    - Be aware of any federal regulations that apply to your industry or business type, such as those related to healthcare, environmental protection, or transportation.

13. **Annual Compliance:**
    - Once registered, stay compliant with ongoing requirements, such as filing annual reports, paying taxes, and renewing licenses.

It's crucial to research and understand the specific requirements and regulations that apply to your business at the federal, state, and local levels. Consult with legal and financial professionals to ensure full compliance and to navigate the registration process smoothly. Additionally, keep accurate records of all registrations, permits, and licenses to avoid legal issues in the future.

4.3 Licenses and Permits

Obtaining the necessary licenses and permits is a crucial step in starting and operating a business legally. The specific licenses and permits you need can vary significantly based on your business type, location, and industry. Here are some common types of licenses and permits that businesses often require:

1. **Business License:**
   - A general business license, often issued by your local city or county government, is required for most businesses. It allows you to operate within a specific jurisdiction.

2. **Federal Employer Identification Number (EIN):**
   - An EIN is required for tax purposes if your business has employees, operates as a corporation or partnership, or meets other IRS criteria.

3. **Sales Tax Permit:**
   - If your business sells products or services subject to sales tax, you may need a sales tax permit or license from your state's Department of Revenue or Taxation.

4. **Health Department Permits:**

- Businesses involved in food service, hospitality, or healthcare typically need health department permits to ensure compliance with health and safety regulations.

5. **Professional Licenses:**
   - Professionals in fields such as law, medicine, engineering, and real estate may need state-issued professional licenses.

6. **Building and Zoning Permits:**
   - Construction and renovation projects often require building permits, and your business location must comply with zoning regulations.

7. **Environmental Permits:**
   - Certain industries, such as manufacturing and energy, may need environmental permits to ensure compliance with environmental regulations.
   - **Alcohol and Tobacco Permits:**
   - Businesses that sell alcoholic beverages or tobacco products typically require special permits and licenses from federal, state, and local authorities.

8. **Fire Department Permits:**
   - Fire department permits may be necessary for businesses to ensure compliance with fire safety codes.

9. **Signage Permits:**
   - Some jurisdictions require permits for outdoor signs, billboards, or other advertising displays.

10. **Home-Based Business Permits:**
    - If you operate a business from your home, you may need specific permits or zoning clearance, depending on local regulations.

11. **Transportation Permits:**
    - Businesses involved in transportation or logistics may require permits for vehicles, routes, or specific types of cargo.

12. **Entertainment and Event Permits:**
    - If your business hosts events, concerts, or other forms of entertainment, you may need special event permits.

13. **Childcare and Education Licenses:**
    - Businesses in childcare, tutoring, or education often require licenses and permits to ensure child safety and educational quality.

14. **Import/Export Licenses:**

- Businesses involved in international trade may need import and export licenses to comply with customs and trade regulations.

15. Home Improvement Contractor Licenses:
- Contractors involved in home improvement or construction may need licenses to operate legally.

16. Tattoo and Piercing Studio Licenses:
- Tattoo parlors and piercing studios typically require permits to ensure health and safety standards are met.

17. Special Use Permits:
- Some businesses or events may require special use permits for activities that are not covered by standard licenses.

To determine which licenses and permits your business needs, research the requirements specific to your industry and location. You can contact your local government's business licensing department, use online resources, or consult with legal and regulatory experts for guidance. Keep in mind that failing to obtain the necessary licenses and permits can result in legal penalties, fines, and business disruptions, so it's essential to prioritize compliance.

4.4 Intellectual Property Protection

Intellectual property (IP) protection is crucial for individuals and businesses that create original works, inventions, or innovative ideas. IP laws provide legal safeguards to protect these creations and give their creators exclusive rights to use and profit from them. There are several forms of intellectual property protection, including patents, trademarks, copyrights, and trade secrets. Here's an overview of each:

1. **Patents:**
   - **Purpose:** Patents protect inventions and innovations, providing exclusive rights to make, use, and sell the patented product or process for a specified period (usually 20 years).
   - **Eligibility:** Inventions must be novel, non-obvious, and useful to be eligible for patent protection.
   - **Application Process:** To obtain a patent, inventors must file a detailed patent application with the relevant patent office, such as the United States Patent and Trademark Office (USPTO). The application typically includes a description of the invention and how it works.

- **Benefits:** Patents can be valuable assets, offering a competitive advantage by preventing others from making, using, or selling the patented invention.

2. **Trademarks:**
   - **Purpose:** Trademarks protect brand names, logos, slogans, and symbols that identify and distinguish products or services in the marketplace.
   - **Eligibility:** Trademarks must be distinctive, not generic, and should not cause confusion with existing trademarks.
   - **Registration:** Trademarks can be registered with the appropriate government agency (e.g., USPTO in the United States). Registration provides legal protection and exclusive rights to use the mark in connection with specific goods or services.
   - **Benefits:** Trademarks help build brand recognition and protect against others using similar marks to confuse consumers.

3. **Copyrights:**
   - **Purpose:** Copyrights protect original works of authorship, such as literary, artistic, and musical creations.
   - **Eligibility:** Works are automatically protected by copyright as soon as they are created and fixed in a tangible medium. No formal registration is required for copyright protection.
   - **Registration:** While not required, copyright registration with the U.S. Copyright Office (or the relevant agency in other countries) provides additional legal benefits, such as the ability to sue for damages in case of infringement.
   - **Benefits:** Copyrights grant creators exclusive rights to reproduce, distribute, and publicly display their work. This protection applies for the lifetime of the creator plus an additional 70 years.

4. **Trade Secrets:**
   - **Purpose:** Trade secrets protect confidential and valuable business information, such as formulas, processes, customer lists, and marketing strategies.
   - **Eligibility:** Information must be genuinely secret, have commercial value, and be subject to reasonable efforts to maintain its secrecy.

- **Protection:** Unlike patents, trademarks, and copyrights, trade secrets do not require formal registration. Protection is based on keeping the information confidential.
- **Benefits:** Trade secret protection can be indefinite as long as the information remains secret. Trade secrets can be crucial for maintaining a competitive advantage.

It's essential to understand the different forms of intellectual property protection and determine which ones apply to your specific creations or innovations. Consulting with legal professionals specializing in intellectual property can help you navigate the complex process of applying for and enforcing IP rights. Proper IP protection can safeguard your assets, promote innovation, and support the growth of your business or creative endeavors.

4.5 Contracts and Agreements

Contracts and agreements are legally binding documents that outline the rights, responsibilities, and obligations of parties involved in a business or personal relationship. Creating well-drafted contracts is essential to prevent disputes and provide clarity in various transactions. Here are some key aspects to consider when dealing with contracts and agreements:

1. **Essential Elements of a Contract:**
   - **Offer:** One party must make a clear and specific offer.
   - **Acceptance:** The other party must agree to the terms of the offer.
   - **Consideration:** Both parties must exchange something of value, such as money, goods, or services.
   - **Legal Purpose:** The contract's purpose must be legal and not violate any laws or public policy.
   - **Capacity:** All parties entering the contract must have the legal capacity to do so (e.g., adults of sound mind).
2. **Types of Contracts:**
   - **Express Contracts:** The terms and conditions are explicitly stated, either in writing or verbally.
   - **Implied Contracts:** The agreement is not explicitly stated but is inferred from the parties' actions or conduct.
   - **Unilateral Contracts:** One party makes a promise in exchange for a specific action or performance from the other party.

- **Bilateral Contracts:** Both parties make promises to each other (a mutual exchange of promises).
3. **Written vs. Oral Contracts:**
   - While oral contracts can be legally binding in many cases, it's generally advisable to have important agreements in writing to provide clarity and evidence of the terms.
4. **Key Contract Clauses:**
   - Parties' Information: Clearly identify all parties involved, including their legal names and contact information.
   - **Scope of Work or Services:** Describe in detail what each party is expected to do or deliver.
   - **Payment Terms:** Specify the payment amount, schedule, and method.
   - **Term and Termination:** Define the duration of the agreement and the conditions under which it can be terminated.
   - **Confidentiality:** If applicable, include provisions to protect sensitive information.
   - **Indemnification and Liability:** Clarify each party's responsibility for losses, damages, or liabilities.
   - **Dispute Resolution:** Outline how disputes will be resolved, such as through arbitration or mediation.
   - **Governing Law:** Specify the state or country laws that will govern the contract.
   - **Force Majeure:** Include clauses that address unforeseeable events that may prevent parties from fulfilling their obligations.
   - **Amendment and Modification:** Describe how the contract can be changed or updated.
5. **Consult with Legal Counsel:**
   - For complex contracts or those with significant financial implications, it's advisable to consult with an attorney who specializes in contract law. They can help you draft, review, and negotiate contracts to protect your interests.
6. **Signing and Execution:**
   - Ensure that all parties sign the contract and keep copies for reference. Some contracts may require notarization or witnesses, depending on local laws and the nature of the agreement.
7. **Performance and Compliance:**

- Once the contract is in effect, both parties must fulfill their obligations as outlined in the agreement. Regularly review and track compliance to avoid potential issues.

8. **Record Keeping:**
   - Maintain copies of all contracts and related correspondence in an organized manner for future reference and potential disputes.

9. **Review Periodically:**
   - It's a good practice to periodically review and update contracts to ensure they remain relevant and in compliance with current laws and business practices.

Remember that the specific requirements and legal principles governing contracts may vary by jurisdiction and the nature of the agreement. When in doubt, seek legal advice to ensure your contracts are legally sound and enforceable.

Funding your business is a crucial step in its development and growth. There are various options available to entrepreneurs and business owners to secure the necessary capital to start, operate, or expand their businesses. Here are some common ways to fund a business:

1. **Bootstrapping:** Bootstrapping involves using your own savings or personal funds to start and run your business. While this may limit your initial resources, it gives you full control over your company and avoids taking on debt or giving away equity.
2. **Family and Friends:** Some entrepreneurs seek financial support from family members or close friends who believe in their business idea. This can be a more flexible and informal way to raise capital but should be approached with caution to maintain personal relationships.
3. **Angel Investors:** Angel investors are individuals who provide capital to early-stage startups in exchange for equity ownership. They often bring industry expertise and connections in addition to funding.
4. **Venture Capital:** Venture capital firms invest in high-growth startups with the potential for significant returns. In exchange for their investment, they typically require equity and may also demand a significant level of control and involvement in the company.

5. **Crowdfunding:** Crowdfunding platforms like Kickstarter, Indiegogo, and GoFundMe allow businesses to raise funds from a large number of people who contribute small amounts of money. This is often used for product launches and creative projects.

6. **Bank Loans:** Traditional bank loans, such as term loans, lines of credit, or Small Business Administration (SBA) loans, can provide capital for businesses. However, they often require a solid credit history and collateral.

7. **Online Lenders:** Online lenders, like LendingClub and OnDeck, offer alternative financing options, such as short-term loans, invoice financing, and merchant cash advances. These can be easier to obtain but may come with higher interest rates.

8. **Business Incubators and Accelerators:** These programs provide funding, mentorship, and resources to startups in exchange for equity. They often culminate in a pitch event where startups present their businesses to potential investors.

9. **Corporate Partnerships:** Some businesses partner with larger corporations that provide funding or resources in exchange for access to innovative ideas, technology, or strategic benefits.

10. **Government Grants and Subsidies:** Depending on your location and industry, there may be government grants, subsidies, or tax incentives available to help fund your business. These often have specific eligibility criteria.

11. **Self-Financing with Profits:** As your business grows, you can reinvest profits to fund further expansion or operations. This is a sustainable way to finance your business over time.

12. **Convertible Notes and SAFE Agreements:** These are debt-like instruments commonly used in early-stage startup financing. They allow investors to convert their investment into equity at a future funding round.

13. **Initial Public Offering (IPO):** Going public through an IPO is an option for established companies with a proven track record. It involves selling shares to the public for the first time.

Selecting the right funding option depends on your business's stage, financial needs, and goals. It's essential to thoroughly research each option, understand its implications, and consult with financial advisors or mentors to make informed decisions. Additionally, having a well-thought-out business plan and financial projections can increase your chances of securing funding from investors or lenders.

5.1 Self-Funding

Self-funding, also known as bootstrapping, is a method of financing your business using your own personal savings, resources, or revenue generated by the business itself. It involves starting and growing your business without relying on external sources of capital, such as loans or investments from others. Here are some key points to consider when self-funding your business:

1. **Personal Savings:** Self-funding often begins with using your personal savings to cover initial startup costs. This can include using your own money from savings accounts, retirement funds, or other personal assets. Using personal savings allows you to maintain full control of your business without incurring debt.

2. **Revenue Generation:** As your business begins to operate, it should ideally generate revenue that can be reinvested to fund further growth. This can include using profits to purchase equipment, hire employees, or expand operations. Reinvesting profits back into the business can lead to organic growth without the need for external financing.

3. **Cost Control:** One of the key principles of self-funding is careful cost management. You need to prioritize spending only on essential expenses and avoid unnecessary overhead. Keeping costs in check helps maximize the funds available for business growth.

4. **Bootstrapping Techniques:** In addition to personal savings and revenue reinvestment, entrepreneurs often employ various bootstrapping techniques to save money and operate efficiently. These can include working from home, using open-source software, bartering services, and outsourcing tasks when necessary.

5. **Lean Startup Approach:** The lean startup methodology emphasizes building a minimum viable product (MVP) to test the market with minimal resources. This approach allows you to validate your business idea and gather customer feedback before committing significant capital.

6. **Alternative Financing:** While self-funding primarily relies on personal resources and revenue, some entrepreneurs combine it with alternative financing options, such as crowdfunding or small loans, to bridge gaps in funding when necessary.

7. **Risk Management:** Self-funding involves taking on personal financial risk. It's important to assess your risk tolerance and have a backup plan in case your business encounters unexpected challenges or requires more capital than initially anticipated.
8. **Gradual Growth:** Self-funding often results in gradual growth, which may be slower compared to businesses that receive significant external funding. However, it allows you to maintain ownership and avoid diluting equity.
9. **Financial Discipline:** Managing your business's finances diligently is crucial when self-funding. Keep accurate financial records, monitor cash flow, and create a budget to ensure your resources are allocated effectively.
10. **Seeking Expert Advice:** Consider seeking advice from mentors, business advisors, or financial professionals who can provide guidance on managing your business's finances and growth strategy.

Self-funding can be a viable option for entrepreneurs who want to retain full control of their businesses and avoid the obligations and potential dilution of equity associated with external financing. However, it may require patience, discipline, and careful financial planning to succeed in the long run.

5.2 Bootstrapping

Bootstrapping is a method of starting and growing a business with minimal external capital, relying primarily on your own resources, personal savings, and revenue generated by the business itself. The term "bootstrapping" comes from the phrase "pulling oneself up by one's bootstraps," which implies self-reliance and self-sufficiency. Bootstrapping is often used by entrepreneurs who want to maintain full control over their businesses and avoid taking on debt or giving away equity to investors. Here are some key aspects of bootstrapping:

1. **Personal Savings:** Bootstrappers often use their personal savings to cover initial startup costs. This can include using funds from savings accounts, retirement accounts, or other personal assets.
2. **Revenue Generation:** The business is expected to generate revenue from its operations, which is reinvested back into the company to fund growth. This revenue can come from selling products or services to customers.

3. **Cost Control:** A significant aspect of bootstrapping is tight control over expenses. Entrepreneurs prioritize spending only on essential items and avoid unnecessary overhead. This might mean working from home, using open-source software, or outsourcing tasks when necessary.
4. **Lean Startup Principles:** Bootstrappers often follow the principles of the lean startup methodology. This approach involves creating a minimum viable product (MVP) to test the market, gather customer feedback, and iterate on the product or service based on that feedback.
5. **Alternative Financing:** While bootstrapping primarily relies on personal resources and revenue, some entrepreneurs use alternative financing options, such as crowdfunding, small loans, or grants, to supplement their bootstrap funding when needed.
6. **Incremental Growth:** Bootstrapped businesses typically experience gradual, incremental growth. This approach may result in slower growth compared to businesses that receive external funding but allows the entrepreneur to maintain ownership and control.
7. **Risk Management:** Entrepreneurs who bootstrap their businesses take on personal financial risk. It's important to assess your risk tolerance and have contingency plans in case the business encounters challenges or requires additional capital.
8. **Resourcefulness:** Bootstrappers often need to be resourceful and creative in finding ways to solve problems and meet their business goals without significant financial resources.
9. **Financial Discipline:** Effective financial management is crucial when bootstrapping. Keeping accurate financial records, monitoring cash flow, and creating a budget can help ensure that resources are used efficiently.
10. **Long-Term Sustainability:** Bootstrapping can lead to a sustainable, long-term business model that is not reliant on external funding. This can be appealing to entrepreneurs who want to build a business gradually and independently.

Bootstrapping can be a rewarding way to start and grow a business, but it requires careful financial planning, discipline, and a willingness to start small and scale gradually. It's important to assess whether bootstrapping is a suitable approach for your business idea and your personal financial situation.

5.3 Seeking Investors

Seeking investors is a common strategy for raising capital to start, expand, or scale a business. Investors provide funds in exchange for ownership equity or a promise of future returns. Here are the key steps and considerations when seeking investors for your business:

1. **Prepare Your Business:** Before seeking investors, ensure that your business concept is well-developed and that you have a solid business plan. This plan should outline your business model, target market, financial projections, and growth strategy.
2. **Identify Your Funding Needs:** Determine how much capital you need and how you plan to use the funds. Be specific about what the investment will be used for, whether it's product development, marketing, expansion, or another purpose.
3. **Know Your Investor Options:**
   - **Angel Investors:** These individuals invest their own money in startups and early-stage companies. They often provide not only capital but also mentorship and industry expertise.
   - **Venture Capitalists (VCs):** Venture capital firms invest in high-growth startups in exchange for equity ownership. VCs typically focus on businesses with significant growth potential and often require a board seat or a say in the company's operations.
   - **Private Equity:** Private equity investors typically invest in more established companies and often seek a controlling stake. They may provide funding for expansion, acquisitions, or restructuring.
   - **Crowdfunding:** Platforms like Kickstarter, Indiegogo, and equity crowdfunding sites allow you to raise funds from a large number of individuals who contribute small amounts. Equity crowdfunding involves selling shares of your company to backers.
   - **Strategic Investors:** These investors are often corporations or industry players who invest in startups that align with their strategic goals. In addition to capital, they may offer access to distribution channels, partnerships, or industry knowledge.

4. **Build a Pitch Deck:** Create a compelling pitch deck that highlights your business, its value proposition, market opportunity, financial projections, and the investment opportunity. Your pitch should be clear, concise, and engaging.
5. **Network:** Building relationships with potential investors is critical. Attend networking events, join industry associations, and seek introductions through your network. Platforms like LinkedIn can also be useful for connecting with potential investors.
6. **Pitch Your Business:** When you identify potential investors, reach out and request a meeting to pitch your business. Be prepared to explain your business and your funding needs concisely. Customize your pitch to address the specific interests and goals of each investor.
7. **Due Diligence:** Expect investors to conduct due diligence on your business. They will scrutinize your financials, market research, team, and business model. Be transparent and ready to provide any requested information.
8. **Negotiate Terms:** If an investor expresses interest, you'll need to negotiate the terms of the investment. This includes discussing the amount of equity or ownership stake the investor will receive, the valuation of your company, and any terms and conditions.
9. **Legal Documentation:** Once you reach an agreement, legal documents will need to be drafted and signed, such as investment agreements and shareholder agreements. It's advisable to consult with legal and financial professionals to ensure the terms are fair and compliant with relevant regulations.
10. **Manage the Relationship:** After securing investment, maintain open communication with your investors and provide regular updates on your business's progress. Investors often expect to be involved in key decisions and may offer guidance and support.

Seeking investors can be a complex process, but it can provide the necessary capital to fuel your business's growth. Be patient and persistent, and remember that finding the right investors who align with your vision and goals is essential for long-term success.

5.4 Crowdfunding

Crowdfunding is a method of raising capital for a project, business, or cause by soliciting small contributions from a large number of people, typically via the internet. It's a popular alternative financing option that allows entrepreneurs, artists, nonprofits, and individuals to access funds and engage with a broader audience. Here are the key elements of crowdfunding:

1. **Types of Crowdfunding:**
   - **Rewards-Based Crowdfunding:** In rewards-based crowdfunding, backers receive non-equity rewards or perks in return for their contributions. These perks can include the product being developed, early access, or other incentives.
   - **Equity Crowdfunding:** Equity crowdfunding involves raising capital by selling shares or ownership stakes in your company to a large number of investors. This type of crowdfunding is subject to securities regulations and may involve more complex legal processes.
   - **Debt Crowdfunding:** Debt crowdfunding, also known as peer-to-peer lending, allows individuals or businesses to borrow money from a group of people in exchange for paying back the principal amount plus interest over time.
   - **Donation-Based Crowdfunding:** In donation-based crowdfunding, contributors give money to support a cause, project, or charitable endeavor without expecting any financial return or reward.
2. **Popular Crowdfunding Platforms:** There are several crowdfunding platforms that cater to different types of crowdfunding campaigns. Some well-known platforms include Kickstarter, Indiegogo, GoFundMe, Patreon (for ongoing support), Crowdfunder (for equity crowdfunding), and Kiva (for microloans).
3. **Setting Funding Goals:** When launching a crowdfunding campaign, you'll need to set a funding goal, which represents the amount of money you need to achieve your project or business objectives. It's essential to set a realistic goal that covers your expenses while motivating potential backers.
4. **Creating a Compelling Campaign:** A successful crowdfunding campaign requires a compelling pitch. This includes a detailed description of your project, clear explanations of how the funds will be used, engaging visuals, and enticing rewards or perks for backers. Storytelling is crucial to connect with potential supporters emotionally.

5. **Marketing and Promotion:** Promoting your crowdfunding campaign is crucial for success. Share your campaign through social media, email newsletters, and personal networks. Engage with your backers, answer their questions, and update them on your progress regularly.
6. **Timing:** The timing of your campaign can influence its success. Consider factors like holidays, industry trends, and the length of your campaign when deciding when to launch.
7. **Fulfillment and Delivery:** Once your campaign is funded, it's important to fulfill your promises to backers, whether that means delivering products, providing updates, or delivering on the campaign's objectives. Maintaining transparency and fulfilling obligations is vital for building trust.
8. **Legal and Tax Considerations:** Be aware of the legal and tax implications of crowdfunding in your jurisdiction. Depending on the type of crowdfunding and your location, you may need to comply with securities laws, report income, and pay taxes on funds received.
9. **Post-Campaign Engagement:** Continue engaging with your backers even after the campaign ends. They can become loyal customers, supporters, and advocates for your business or cause.
10. **Learn from Feedback:** Analyze your campaign's performance and gather feedback from backers to improve future campaigns. Learning from both successes and failures is essential for growing your crowdfunding skills.

Crowdfunding can be an effective way to access capital, validate your business idea, and build a community of supporters. However, it's important to approach crowdfunding with careful planning, a compelling story, and a strong marketing strategy to increase your chances of success.

5.5 Small Business Loans

Small business loans are financial products designed to provide funding to small and medium-sized businesses (SMEs) to help them start, operate, or expand their operations. These loans come in various forms and are typically offered by banks, credit unions, online lenders, and government agencies. Here are some key points to consider when seeking small business loans:

1. **Types of Small Business Loans:**
   - **Term Loans:** Term loans are a common type of business loan with a fixed repayment schedule and interest rate. They are used for various purposes, such as purchasing equipment, financing working capital, or expanding the business.
   - **Lines of Credit:** A business line of credit provides access to a predetermined amount of funds that can be drawn upon as needed. Interest is only paid on the amount borrowed, making it a flexible financing option.
   - **SBA Loans:** The U.S. Small Business Administration (SBA) offers various loan programs to assist small businesses, including 7(a) loans, 504 loans, and microloans. These loans often have more favorable terms and lower interest rates but may require more documentation and have longer approval times.
   - **Equipment Financing:** This type of loan is used specifically to purchase equipment or machinery for your business. The equipment itself often serves as collateral for the loan.
   - **Invoice Financing:** Invoice financing, or factoring, allows businesses to receive immediate cash by selling their unpaid invoices to a third-party lender at a discount.
   - **Merchant Cash Advances:** Merchant cash advances provide a lump sum of capital in exchange for a percentage of your daily credit card sales. Repayments are made through a portion of your daily credit card transactions.
2. **Eligibility Criteria:** Lenders typically consider factors such as your credit score, business revenue, time in business, and financial stability when evaluating your eligibility for a loan. Requirements may vary depending on the lender and the type of loan.
3. **Interest Rates and Fees:** Different lenders offer loans with varying interest rates and fee structures. Be sure to compare rates and fees to find the most cost-effective loan option for your business.
4. **Loan Terms:** Loan terms refer to the repayment period and frequency of payments. Longer loan terms may result in lower monthly payments but can also mean higher overall interest costs.
5. **Collateral:** Some business loans require collateral, such as real estate, inventory, or equipment, to secure the loan. Unsecured loans do not require collateral but may have higher interest rates.

6. **Business Plan and Documentation:** Many lenders will require a detailed business plan, financial statements, tax returns, and other documentation to assess your business's creditworthiness.
7. **Government Assistance:** Check if your business qualifies for government-backed loans or grants, such as those offered by the Small Business Administration in the United States. These programs often provide more favorable terms and lower interest rates.
8. **Online Lenders:** Online lenders have become increasingly popular and offer a streamlined application process. However, be cautious and thoroughly research online lenders to ensure they are reputable and offer fair terms.
9. **Loan Use:** Specify how you intend to use the loan funds in your loan application. Lenders often want to know how the capital will be used to assess the viability of your business plan.
10. **Repayment Plan:** Develop a solid repayment plan to ensure you can comfortably meet your loan obligations. Failure to repay loans can result in damaging your credit and potentially losing assets if collateral is involved.

Before applying for a small business loan, it's essential to assess your business's financial needs and ability to repay the debt. Shop around for the best loan terms and consider seeking advice from financial advisors or business consultants to make informed decisions.

Building your business brand is a crucial aspect of establishing a strong presence in the marketplace and creating a lasting impression on your target audience. Here are some key steps to help you build and develop your business brand:

1. **Define Your Brand Identity:**
   - Start by defining your brand's mission, values, and unique selling proposition (USP). What sets your business apart from the competition?
2. **Know Your Target Audience:**
   - Understand your target market's demographics, preferences, and pain points. Tailor your brand to resonate with their needs and desires.
3. **Create a Memorable Logo and Visual Identity:**
   - Design a professional and eye-catching logo that represents your brand. Consistency in color schemes, fonts, and imagery across all platforms is essential.
4. **Craft Your Brand Message:**
   - Develop a clear and concise brand message that communicates your value proposition. Use this message consistently in all your marketing materials.
5. **Build a Strong Online Presence:**

- Create a website that reflects your brand's identity and is user-friendly. Optimize it for search engines (SEO) to increase visibility. Establish a presence on social media platforms relevant to your audience.

6. **Content Marketing:**
   - Share valuable and relevant content that aligns with your brand message. This includes blog posts, videos, and infographics.

7. **Leverage Social Media:**
   - Use social media platforms to engage with your audience. Respond to comments and messages, and use these channels to showcase your brand's personality.

8. **Consistent Branding:**
   - Maintain consistency across all touchpoints, from your website and social media to business cards and product packaging.

9. **Customer Service:**
   - Ensure your customer service aligns with your brand's values and promises. Happy customers can become brand advocates.

10. **Partnerships and Collaborations:**
    - Partner with other businesses or influencers that align with your brand values to expand your reach and credibility.

11. **Monitor Your Reputation:**
    - Keep an eye on reviews, comments, and mentions of your brand online. Address negative feedback and capitalize on positive reviews.

12. **Adapt and Evolve:**
    - As your business grows, be willing to adapt and evolve your brand to stay relevant. Stay up to date with industry trends and customer preferences.

13. **Legal Protection:**

    - Consider trademarking your brand name and logo to protect your intellectual property.

14. **Measure and Analyze:**
    - Use tools like Google Analytics and social media insights to track the performance of your branding efforts. Adjust your strategy based on the data.

15. **Employee Branding:**

- Ensure that your employees understand and embody your brand. Their interactions with customers and the public should reflect your brand's values.

16. Community Engagement:
- Get involved in your community through charitable activities or local events. This can strengthen your brand's local presence.

Building a brand is an ongoing process that requires time and effort. It's not just about visuals but also about the experience and emotions associated with your business. A strong and consistent brand will help you connect with your target audience, build trust, and ultimately drive business success.

6.1 Branding Basics

Branding is a fundamental element of marketing and business strategy that involves creating a distinct and memorable identity for your business or product. Here are some branding basics to help you understand and get started with branding:

1. **Brand Definition:**
   - A brand is more than just a logo or a name. It encompasses the overall perception and reputation of your business, including its values, mission, and personality.
2. **Branding Components:**
   - Branding consists of various components, including your logo, color scheme, typography, tagline, messaging, and overall design elements. These should be consistent across all your marketing materials.
3. **Target Audience:**
   - Your brand should be tailored to appeal to your specific target audience. Understand their demographics, needs, and preferences to create a brand that resonates with them.
4. **Unique Selling Proposition (USP):**
   - Your brand should highlight what sets your business apart from the competition. What unique value do you offer to customers?
5. **Brand Values:**
   - Determine the core values and principles that guide your business. These values should be reflected in your branding and decision-making.
6. **Visual Identity:**

- Design a memorable and visually appealing logo, along with a consistent color palette and typography. These elements should represent your brand and be instantly recognizable.

7. **Brand Messaging:**
   - Develop a clear and compelling brand message that communicates your USP and values. This message should be used consistently in all your marketing materials and communications.

8. **Consistency:**
   - Maintain consistency in all branding elements across different platforms, from your website and social media to physical materials like business cards and packaging.

9. **Customer Experience:**
   - The customer's experience with your brand is a critical part of branding. Ensure that every interaction with your business reinforces your brand's values and promises.

10. **Market Research:**
    - Conduct research to understand your competitors, industry trends, and customer preferences. This information can help you refine your branding strategy.

11. **Brand Positioning:**
    - Define where your brand stands in the market. Are you the affordable option, the premium choice, or something else? Your positioning should align with your target audience's expectations.

12. **Brand Storytelling:**
    - Use storytelling to convey your brand's history, mission, and values. Share the story of how your business came to be and why it matters.

13. **Brand Guidelines:**
    - Create a set of brand guidelines that outline how your branding elements should be used. This helps maintain consistency when working with different designers and marketers.

14. **Emotional Connection:**
    - Good branding should evoke emotions and create a connection with your audience. People are more likely to remember and engage with brands that make them feel something.

15. **Adapt and Evolve:**

- Be open to adapting your brand as your business grows and as market conditions change. A brand that is too rigid may become outdated.

16. Legal Considerations:
- Protect your brand by registering trademarks and other intellectual property as necessary to prevent others from using your brand elements.

Branding is an ongoing process that requires careful planning and execution. It plays a critical role in building trust and loyalty among your customers, making it a valuable asset for your business's long-term success.

6.2 Logo and Visual Identity

Creating a compelling logo and visual identity is a crucial aspect of branding. Your logo and visual identity are often the first things people notice about your brand, and they play a significant role in forming a lasting impression. Here's a breakdown of how to design a logo and establish a visual identity for your brand:

1. **Logo Design:**
   - **Simplicity:** Keep your logo simple and easily recognizable. Complex logos can be difficult to remember.
   - **Memorability:** A great logo is memorable. It should leave a lasting impression on those who see it.
   - **Relevance:** Your logo should reflect your business and its values. It should resonate with your target audience.
   - **Versatility:** Ensure your logo looks good in different sizes and across various media, from digital platforms to printed materials.
   - **Uniqueness:** Your logo should be distinct from competitors to avoid confusion and establish your brand's individuality.
   - **Timelessness:** Aim for a design that won't look outdated in a few years. Avoid trends that may quickly go out of style.
   - **Scalability:** Your logo should look good when scaled up or down, whether on a billboard or a business card.
2. **Color Scheme:**
   - Choose a color palette that aligns with your brand's personality and values.

- Consider the psychology of colors. Different colors can evoke specific emotions and associations. For example, blue often conveys trust and reliability, while red can symbolize passion or excitement.
- Select primary and secondary colors to create visual hierarchy and balance in your design.

3. **Typography:**
   - Choose fonts that are easy to read and fit your brand's personality. The typeface you select should complement your logo and overall design.
   - Use different fonts for headers, subheadings, and body text to create a consistent and visually appealing hierarchy.

4. **Imagery:**
   - If your brand uses imagery, ensure it aligns with your brand's message and values. Select images that resonate with your target audience.
   - Consider using original photography or illustrations to make your brand more unique.

5. **Design Elements:**
   - Incorporate design elements such as lines, shapes, and patterns to create a cohesive visual identity.
   - These elements can help reinforce your brand's personality and message when used consistently.

6. **Brand Guidelines:**
   - Create a set of brand guidelines that outline how your visual identity elements should be used. This document should detail specifications for logo usage, color codes, font choices, and design rules.
   - Brand guidelines help maintain consistency across all brand materials, both in-house and when working with designers or marketing teams.

7. **Testing and Feedback:**
   - Before finalizing your logo and visual identity, seek feedback from peers, colleagues, or potential customers. Testing your design with a small audience can help you make improvements and identify any potential issues.

8. **Professional Help:**

- If you're not confident in your design skills, consider hiring a professional graphic designer. They can bring expertise and creativity to the process.

Remember that your logo and visual identity are a long-term investment in your brand. It's often worth spending time and resources to get them right, as they play a pivotal role in how your audience perceives your business.

6.3 Creating a Unique Value Proposition

Creating a unique value proposition (UVP) is essential for your business to stand out in a competitive market. Your UVP is a clear and compelling statement that communicates the unique benefits and value your products or services offer to your target audience. Here's how to create a unique value proposition:

1. **Understand Your Target Audience:**
   - Start by thoroughly understanding your target market. What are their needs, problems, desires, and preferences? What do they value the most when choosing products or services?
2. **Analyze the Competition:**
   - Research your competitors to see what they are offering and how they are positioning themselves. Identify gaps and opportunities where you can differentiate.
3. **Identify Your Unique Features and Benefits:**
   - Determine what sets your products or services apart from the competition. This could be a unique feature, exceptional quality, pricing, convenience, or a combination of factors.
4. **Solve a Problem or Meet a Need:**
   - Your UVP should address a specific problem or need that your target audience has. How does your product or service make their lives better, easier, or more enjoyable?
5. **Make It Clear and Concise:**
   - Your UVP should be clear and concise, typically expressed in a single sentence or a short paragraph. Avoid jargon or complicated language. It should be easily understood by your audience.
6. **Highlight Benefits Over Features:**
   - Focus on the benefits your product or service provides rather than just its features. Benefits explain how your offering

improves the customer's life, while features describe what it does.

7. **Use Compelling Language:**
   - Use strong, persuasive language in your UVP. Make it emotional and relatable to your audience. Consider using power words that evoke a response.

8. **Be Specific:**
   - Avoid vague statements. Provide specific details about what customers can expect. If you offer faster shipping, quantify it ("Get your order in 24 hours") or use specific numbers to highlight cost savings or performance improvements.

9. **Test and Refine:**
   - Once you've crafted your UVP, test it with your target audience and gather feedback. Refine it based on their reactions and suggestions. Your UVP should resonate with your audience.

10. **Consistency:**
    - Ensure your UVP aligns with your branding and is consistently communicated across all your marketing materials, website, and customer interactions.

11. **Continuously Update:**
    - As your business evolves or market conditions change, be prepared to update your UVP to stay relevant and competitive.

12. **Deliver on Your Promise:**
    - Your UVP is not just a marketing slogan; it's a promise to your customers. Ensure that your product or service lives up to the expectations you've set with your UVP.

Here are a few examples of strong UVPs from well-known companies:

- **Apple:** "Think different."
- **Amazon:** "Earth's biggest selection."
- **Lyft:** "Rides in minutes."

Your UVP should be authentic and true to your business, reflecting what you can genuinely deliver to your customers. A well-crafted UVP can be a powerful tool for attracting and retaining customers.

Creating a strong online and offline presence for your business is essential for reaching and engaging with a diverse audience. The two complement each other and can significantly impact your brand's success. Here's how to manage both effectively:

1. **Online Presence:**

Website: Your website is your online headquarters. Make sure it's well-designed, user-friendly, and optimized for search engines (SEO). Your website should provide essential information about your business, products, services, and contact details.

- **Social Media:** Establish a presence on social media platforms relevant to your target audience. Regularly post engaging content, interact with your followers, and use social media to drive traffic to your website.
- **Content Marketing:** Create valuable content, such as blog posts, videos, and infographics, that addresses the needs and interests of your target audience. This content can help establish you as an authority in your industry and attract organic traffic.
- **Email Marketing:** Build and maintain an email list. Send newsletters, promotions, and updates to your subscribers. Personalize your emails and use segmentation to make them more relevant to different audience segments.
- **Online Advertising:** Use online advertising platforms like Google Ads and social media advertising to reach a broader audience and target specific demographics.
- **Online Reviews and Reputation Management:** Encourage satisfied customers to leave positive reviews on platforms like Google My Business and Yelp. Respond to both positive and negative reviews professionally.
2. **Offline Presence:**
   - **Physical Location:** If you have a physical store, office, or workspace, ensure that it is well-maintained and welcoming. A clean, attractive physical location can make a strong impression on visitors.
   - **Networking:** Attend industry events, trade shows, and local networking events to build connections and promote your

business. Face-to-face interactions can foster trust and credibility.

- **Print Marketing:** Use offline materials like business cards, brochures, flyers, and posters to promote your business. Ensure that these materials are professionally designed and reflect your brand identity.
- **Local Marketing:** Optimize your business for local search by claiming and optimizing your Google My Business listing. Use local SEO strategies to ensure your business appears in local search results.
- **Partnerships:** Partner with other local businesses or organizations that share your target audience. This can help you cross-promote and expand your reach.
- **Direct Mail:** Consider using direct mail campaigns to target specific demographics or areas with your marketing materials.
- **Community Involvement:** Get involved in your community through sponsorships, charity events, or volunteer work. This can help you build goodwill and a positive reputation locally.
- **Trade Shows and Exhibitions:** Participate in industry-specific trade shows and exhibitions to showcase your products or services and connect with potential customers.
- **Media Coverage:** Seek media coverage through press releases, interviews, or news articles. Local newspapers, magazines, and TV stations can help raise your brand's visibility.
- **Branded Merchandise:** Consider creating branded merchandise, such as branded clothing or promotional items, which can serve as both marketing tools and revenue sources.

Balancing your online and offline presence depends on your business goals, target audience, and industry. An effective marketing strategy incorporates both, making sure they are aligned with your brand identity and customer expectations.

M arketing and sales are essential components of any business, and developing effective strategies in these areas is crucial for success. Here are some key strategies for both marketing and sales:

1. **Marketing Strategies:**
    *   **Know Your Target Audience:** Understanding your ideal customers is fundamental. Create buyer personas to identify their needs, preferences, and pain points.
    *   **Content Marketing:** Produce high-quality, relevant content to attract and engage your audience. This includes blog posts, videos, infographics, and more.
    *   **Social Media Marketing:** Utilize social platforms to reach and engage with your audience. Choose the platforms that align with your target demographic.
    *   **Search Engine Optimization (SEO):** Optimize your website and content for search engines to improve visibility and organic traffic.
    *   **Email Marketing:** Build and nurture an email list. Send personalized and relevant content, promotions, and updates to your subscribers.

- **Pay-Per-Click (PPC) Advertising:** Use platforms like Google Ads and Facebook Ads to target specific keywords and demographics with paid advertisements.
- **Influencer Marketing:** Partner with influencers in your industry to reach their audience and build credibility.
- **Referral and Affiliate Marketing:** Encourage your customers to refer others and reward them for successful referrals.
- **Public Relations:** Build relationships with media outlets and influencers to secure press coverage and increase brand visibility.
- **Marketing Automation:** Use tools like HubSpot, Marketo, or Mailchimp to streamline marketing tasks, automate email campaigns, and analyze data.

2. **Sales Strategies:**
   - **Customer Relationship Management (CRM):** Implement a CRM system to manage leads, track interactions, and monitor sales opportunities.
   - **Sales Training:** Continuously train your sales team to improve product knowledge, communication skills, and objection handling.
   - **Lead Qualification:** Develop a clear process for qualifying leads to prioritize efforts on those most likely to convert.
   - **Sales Funnel Optimization:** Analyze and optimize your sales funnel to reduce friction points and improve conversion rates.
   - **Value Selling:** Focus on the value your product or service provides and how it solves your customers' problems.
   - **Sales Enablement:** Equip your sales team with the right tools, content, and resources to sell effectively.
   - **Customer Feedback:** Collect and act on customer feedback to improve your product or service and meet customer needs more effectively.
   - **Sales Metrics:** Track key sales metrics, such as conversion rates, average deal size, and sales cycle length, to identify areas for improvement.
   - **Upselling and Cross-selling:** Maximize revenue from existing customers by offering complementary products or upgrades.

- **Sales Process Automation:** Implement automation tools to streamline routine sales tasks, such as lead scoring and follow-up emails.

Remember, your marketing and sales strategies should align with your overall business goals and adapt to changes in your industry and customer preferences. Regularly measure and analyze the performance of these strategies and be prepared to make adjustments as needed to stay competitive and successful.

7.1 Digital Marketing

Digital marketing encompasses various online strategies and channels to promote products, services, or brands to a digital audience. In today's increasingly connected world, digital marketing is a critical component of a comprehensive marketing strategy. Here are some key elements of digital marketing:

1. **Website:** Your website is often the central hub of your digital marketing efforts. Ensure it is well-designed, mobile-responsive, and optimized for search engines. Your website should provide a positive user experience.
2. **Search Engine Optimization (SEO):** SEO involves optimizing your website and content to rank higher in search engine results pages (SERPs). This increases organic (non-paid) traffic to your site.
3. **Content Marketing:** Create and share valuable, relevant content such as blog posts, articles, videos, infographics, and more. Content marketing helps build your brand's authority and engage your target audience.
4. **Social Media Marketing:** Utilize various social media platforms to connect with your audience, share content, run ads, and build brand awareness. Each platform has its own unique audience and features, so choose the ones that best align with your target demographic.
5. **Email Marketing:** Build and maintain an email list of subscribers interested in your products or services. Send them regular updates, promotions, and valuable content to nurture leads and drive conversions.
6. **Pay-Per-Click (PPC) Advertising:** PPC advertising allows you to create targeted ads that appear at the top of search results or on social media. You pay when users click on your ad. Google Ads and social media platforms like Facebook Ads are popular choices.

7. **Affiliate Marketing:** Partner with affiliates who promote your products or services in exchange for a commission on sales. Affiliate marketing can extend your reach and drive sales.
8. **Influencer Marketing:** Collaborate with influencers in your industry to promote your products or services. Influencers have a dedicated following that trusts their recommendations.
9. **Online Public Relations:** Manage your brand's online reputation by building relationships with media outlets and influencers. Secure press coverage, manage reviews, and respond to customer feedback.
10. **Analytics and Data Analysis:** Use tools like Google Analytics and social media insights to track the performance of your digital marketing efforts. This data helps you refine your strategies and make informed decisions.
11. **Marketing Automation:** Implement marketing automation tools (e.g., HubSpot, Marketo) to streamline marketing tasks, segment your audience, and deliver personalized content to leads and customers.
12. **Mobile Marketing:** Optimize your digital marketing efforts for mobile users, as a significant portion of internet traffic comes from mobile devices. Consider mobile apps, responsive design, and mobile advertising.
13. **Video Marketing:** Leverage the power of video content on platforms like YouTube, Instagram, and TikTok to engage your audience and tell your brand's story.
14. **Chatbots and AI:** Utilize chatbots and artificial intelligence for customer support, lead generation, and personalization on your website and social media.
15. **E-commerce Marketing:** If you sell products online, use e-commerce marketing strategies like cart abandonment emails, product recommendations, and user reviews to boost sales.

Digital marketing is a dynamic field that requires staying up-to-date with the latest trends and tools. The effectiveness of your digital marketing efforts depends on how well you understand your target audience and adapt your strategies to their evolving needs and preferences.

7.2 Content Marketing

Content marketing is a strategic approach to creating and distributing valuable, relevant, and consistent content to attract and engage a clearly defined target audience. The primary goal of content marketing is to build trust, establish authority, and ultimately drive profitable customer actions, such as purchasing a product or service. Here are the key elements of content marketing:

1. **Audience Research:** Understand your target audience, their needs, pain points, and preferences. Develop detailed buyer personas to guide your content creation.
2. **Content Strategy:** Create a content strategy that outlines your goals, the types of content you'll produce (e.g., blog posts, videos, infographics, ebooks), and the channels you'll use to distribute it.
3. **High-Quality Content:** Produce content that is informative, valuable, and well-crafted. Content should address your audience's questions and problems. Focus on delivering real solutions.
4. **Consistency:** Regularly publish content to maintain your audience's interest and trust. Consistency helps establish your brand as a reliable source of information.
5. **Search Engine Optimization (SEO):** Optimize your content for search engines to improve its visibility in search results. This involves keyword research, on-page optimization, and earning backlinks.
6. **Content Distribution:** Promote your content through various channels, including your website, blog, social media, email, and other relevant platforms. Share your content where your target audience is most active.
7. **Social Media Marketing:** Leverage social media platforms to share and promote your content, engage with your audience, and build a community around your brand.
8. **Email Marketing:** Use email to distribute content, nurture leads, and build relationships with your subscribers. Email is a powerful tool for delivering personalized content.
9. **Video Marketing:** Videos have become a popular form of content. Create video content for platforms like YouTube, Instagram, TikTok, and even use live streaming for engagement.
10. **Interactive Content:** Experiment with interactive content such as quizzes, polls, and surveys to engage your audience and gather valuable data.

11. **Guest Posting:** Contribute content to authoritative websites and blogs in your industry to reach new audiences and build backlinks to your site.
12. **Content Repurposing:** Maximize the value of your content by repurposing it into different formats. For example, turn a blog post into a podcast episode or an infographic.
13. **Measurement and Analysis:** Use analytics tools to measure the performance of your content. Track metrics such as website traffic, engagement, conversion rates, and customer retention.
14. **Adaptation:** Continuously adapt your content strategy based on the data and feedback you receive. Experiment with new formats and topics to keep your content fresh and appealing.
15. **Content Calendar:** Create a content calendar to plan and organize your content production and distribution. This ensures that you maintain consistency and cover a variety of topics.

Content marketing is a long-term strategy that requires dedication and patience. The goal is to build a loyal audience and drive profitable actions over time, rather than seeking immediate returns. By providing valuable content that addresses your audience's needs, you can establish your brand as an industry leader and create lasting customer relationships.

7.3 Email Marketing

Email marketing is a powerful digital marketing strategy that involves sending targeted emails to a group of subscribers or potential customers with the goal of building relationships, promoting products or services, and achieving specific business objectives. Here are the key components and best practices for effective email marketing:

1. **Build and Segment Your Email List:**
   - Collect email addresses through sign-up forms on your website, social media, or events.
   - Segment your email list based on factors like demographics, behaviors, and engagement levels to send more personalized content.
2. **Choose the Right Email Marketing Platform:**
   - Use an email marketing platform (e.g., Mailchimp, Constant Contact, or HubSpot) to create, send, and manage your email campaigns.

3. **Create Engaging Content:**
   - Craft compelling subject lines that encourage recipients to open your emails.
   - Provide valuable and relevant content that meets the needs and interests of your subscribers.
   - Include clear and concise calls to action (CTAs) that guide recipients on what to do next.
4. **Design Mobile-Responsive Emails:**
   - Ensure your emails are optimized for mobile devices, as a significant portion of email opens occur on smartphones and tablets.
5. **Personalization:**
   - Use recipient's names and personalize content based on their preferences and behavior.
   - Segment your email list to send tailored content to specific groups of subscribers.
6. **A/B Testing:**
   - Experiment with different email elements, such as subject lines, content, CTAs, and send times, to determine what resonates best with your audience.
7. **Automated Workflows:**
   - Set up automated email workflows for lead nurturing, welcome sequences, abandoned cart recovery, and more to save time and enhance user experience.
8. **Compliance with Regulations:**
   - Comply with email marketing regulations, such as the CAN-SPAM Act or the General Data Protection Regulation (GDPR), and include an unsubscribe option in your emails.
9. **Measure and Analyze:**
   - Use email analytics to track key metrics like open rates, click-through rates, conversion rates, and unsubscribe rates.
   - Analyze the data to understand what's working and what needs improvement.

Engage with Subscribers:

- Encourage subscribers to reply to your emails, ask for feedback, or provide customer support via email.

- Engage with your audience on social media and other digital platforms to foster a sense of community.

10. Timing and Frequency:
- Experiment with the timing and frequency of your email campaigns. Test different days and times to find out when your subscribers are most active.

11. Monitoring and List Hygiene:
- Regularly clean your email list by removing inactive or unengaged subscribers.
- Monitor your sender reputation to ensure your emails are delivered to the inbox rather than the spam folder.

12. Email Marketing Goals:
- Clearly define your email marketing goals, whether it's increasing website traffic, generating leads, boosting sales, or promoting a new product or service.

13. Feedback and Improvements:
- Pay attention to subscriber feedback and make improvements based on their suggestions and preferences.

Email marketing is a cost-effective way to nurture leads, retain customers, and drive conversions. By sending targeted, relevant, and engaging emails to your audience, you can build trust and maintain a strong online presence. Regularly review and adapt your email marketing strategy to ensure it aligns with your business goals and your subscribers' needs.

7.4 Sales Techniques and Strategies

Effective sales techniques and strategies are essential for driving revenue and growing a business. Whether you're in a B2B (business-to-business) or B2C (business-to-consumer) sales environment, these strategies can help you build relationships, close deals, and exceed your sales targets:

1. **Build Relationships:**
   - Relationship Selling: Focus on building genuine, long-term relationships with customers. Understand their needs, preferences, and challenges.
2. **Understand Your Product/Service:**

- **Product Knowledge:** Thoroughly understand your product or service, its features, benefits, and how it solves customer problems.

3. **Effective Communication:**
   - **Active Listening:** Pay close attention to your customers. Understand their pain points and tailor your pitch accordingly.
   - **Effective Communication:** Clearly and persuasively convey your product's value proposition and how it meets the customer's needs.

4. **Prospecting:**
   - **Identify Prospects:** Use research and data analysis to identify potential customers who are likely to benefit from your product or service.

5. **Qualification:**
   - **Lead Qualification:** Prioritize leads based on their potential value and likelihood to buy. Focus your efforts on the most promising prospects.

6. **Sales Process:**
   - **Sales Funnel:** Develop a structured sales process with defined stages, from lead generation to closing the deal.
   - **Closing Techniques:** Use proven closing techniques like the assumptive close, trial close, or the choice close to prompt the customer to make a decision.

7. **Objection Handling:**
   - **Address Objections:** Be prepared to handle objections. Listen to the customer's concerns, provide solutions, and re-emphasize the value of your product.

8. **Follow-Up:**
   - **Persistent Follow-Up:** After initial contact, stay in touch with potential customers. Send relevant content and reminders to keep your product or service top of mind.

9. **Sales Tools:**
   - **Utilize Sales Tools:** Leverage CRM (Customer Relationship Management) software, sales automation, and other sales tools to streamline your efforts.

10. **Team Collaboration:**
    - **Sales Team Collaboration:** Work closely with other members of your sales team and share insights and strategies.

11. Customer-Centric Approach:
- **Customer-Centric Sales:** Focus on delivering value to the customer rather than just making a sale. Be customer-oriented in your approach.

12. Time Management:
- **Effective Time Management:** Prioritize tasks, avoid distractions, and allocate your time efficiently to maximize productivity.

13. Continuous Learning:
- **Sales Training:** Stay up-to-date with sales best practices, attend training sessions, and seek ongoing self-improvement.

14. Adaptability:
- **Adapt to Customer Needs:** Be flexible and adaptable in your sales approach to meet the specific needs and preferences of each customer.

15. Networking:
- **Networking:** Build a strong professional network and leverage it for referrals and new opportunities.

16. Sales Metrics:
- **KPI Tracking:** Measure key performance indicators (KPIs) such as conversion rates, sales cycle length, and revenue, and use this data to make data-driven decisions.

Remember that sales is not just about closing deals; it's about solving problems, meeting needs, and providing value to your customers. An ethical and customer-focused approach to sales is more likely to build trust and lead to long-lasting customer relationships.

Building a successful business team is essential for the growth and sustainability of your company. A well-organized and motivated team can help you achieve your business goals, handle challenges, and drive innovation. Here are steps to build an effective business team:

1. **Define Your Business Goals:**
   - Clearly outline your business objectives and what you want to achieve. Your team's mission and vision should align with these goals.
2. **Identify Team Roles:**
   - Determine the specific roles and responsibilities needed to achieve your goals. Consider what skills, expertise, and qualities are required for each role.
3. **Recruit Talent:**
   - Look for individuals who possess the skills and qualities required for the roles you've identified. Use a variety of recruitment methods, including job postings, networking, and referrals.
4. **Cultivate a Diverse Team:**
   - A diverse team with varying backgrounds, experiences, and perspectives can bring fresh ideas and creativity to your business.

5. **Foster a Positive Company Culture:**
   - Create a company culture that promotes teamwork, respect, and collaboration. Encourage open communication and a supportive work environment.
6. **Set Clear Expectations:**
   - Ensure that team members understand their roles and responsibilities, as well as your expectations for performance and behavior.

Provide Training and Development:

- Invest in ongoing training and development programs to help your team acquire new skills and stay up-to-date with industry trends.

Delegate Authority:

- Trust your team to make decisions and take ownership of their work. Delegating authority empowers team members and encourages accountability.

Establish Effective Communication:

- Regular team meetings, clear communication channels, and feedback mechanisms are crucial for keeping everyone informed and on the same page.

Encourage Innovation:

- Create an environment that allows team members to brainstorm, experiment, and come up with new ideas. Innovation can drive your business forward.
- **Manage Conflict:**
- Conflicts are inevitable in any team. Learn how to address issues constructively and resolve conflicts while keeping the team's goals in mind.

7. **Provide Recognition and Rewards:**
   - Acknowledge and reward your team members for their hard work and achievements. Recognizing their contributions can boost morale and motivation.
8. **Promote Work-Life Balance:**

- Encourage a healthy work-life balance to prevent burnout and maintain long-term productivity.

9. **Regularly Evaluate and Adjust:**
   - Continuously assess the team's performance and make necessary adjustments to roles, processes, and strategies to improve effectiveness.

10. **Lead by Example:**
    - As a leader, set the tone for your team by demonstrating the values and work ethic you expect from them. Be a role model for professionalism and dedication.

11. **Adapt to Changing Needs:**
    - Businesses evolve, and so should your team. Be prepared to adjust your team's composition and strategies to meet changing demands and challenges.

Building a successful business team takes time and effort, but with the right approach, it can be a valuable asset for your organization's success.

8.1 Hiring Your First Employees

Hiring your first employees is a significant step in growing your business. It's crucial to approach this process carefully to ensure you make the right choices. Here's a step-by-step guide to help you hire your first employees:

1. **Define Your Needs:**
   - Start by identifying the specific roles and responsibilities your business requires. Consider the skills, qualifications, and experience needed for each position.

2. **Create Job Descriptions:**
   - Write detailed job descriptions for each role. Include key responsibilities, qualifications, and any specific expectations. This will help potential candidates understand what you're looking for.

3. **Determine Compensation and Benefits:**
   - Decide on the salary, benefits, and any other perks you'll offer to your employees. Research industry standards to ensure your compensation is competitive.

4. **Compliance and Legal Requirements:**

- Familiarize yourself with labor laws and regulations in your area, as well as any specific requirements for hiring and employing people in your industry. This may include tax obligations, workers' compensation, and health insurance.

5. **Recruitment Strategy:**
   - Choose a recruitment strategy that fits your budget and the positions you're trying to fill. Common methods include online job postings, networking, referrals, and local job fairs.

6. **Screen Resumes and Applications:**
   - Review resumes and applications to shortlist candidates who meet your job requirements. Look for relevant experience, skills, and a good cultural fit.

7. **Conduct Interviews:**
   - Interview candidates to assess their skills, qualifications, and compatibility with your company culture. Behavioral interviews and skills tests can help you gauge a candidate's fit for the role.

8. **Check References:**
   - Contact the candidate's references to verify their work history, skills, and reliability. This step is crucial for making informed hiring decisions.

9. **Make an Offer:**
   - Once you've selected a candidate, extend a formal job offer that includes details about compensation, benefits, and any other terms of employment. Be prepared to negotiate if necessary.

10. **Complete Onboarding:**
    - Develop an onboarding process to help new employees adjust to their roles and the company culture. This may include training, orientation, and providing necessary resources.

11. **Provide Clear Expectations:**
    - Communicate your expectations for performance, responsibilities, and behavior to the new employees. This will help set clear boundaries and ensure everyone is on the same page.

12. **Compliance with Legal Documents:**
    - Ensure all necessary legal documents, such as employment contracts and tax forms, are completed accurately. Consult with legal and accounting professionals if needed.

13. **Register for Payroll and Taxes:**

- Set up a payroll system, and ensure you're properly withholding and remitting payroll taxes. This is a critical step to stay in compliance with tax authorities.

14. Maintain Open Communication:
- Encourage open lines of communication with your new employees. Create an environment where they feel comfortable asking questions or addressing concerns.

15. Evaluate and Provide Feedback:
- Establish a performance evaluation process to provide feedback and set goals for your new employees. Regular feedback helps with their development and engagement.

Hiring your first employees is a significant milestone in your business's growth. Take the time to find the right individuals who can help you achieve your company's objectives while contributing positively to your company culture.

8.2 Leadership and Management

Leadership and management are two distinct but interrelated concepts that play vital roles in the success of organizations. While they share some common characteristics, they serve different functions within an organization. Here's a breakdown of leadership and management and their key differences:

1. **Leadership:**
   - **Vision and Inspiration:** Leadership is primarily about setting a vision, inspiring people, and motivating them to work toward a common goal. Leaders focus on the "what" and "why" of an organization.
   - **Influence and Direction:** Leaders use their personal influence and charisma to guide and influence others. They may not have formal authority but can lead through inspiration and example.
   - **Long-Term Perspective:** Leaders often take a long-term perspective, looking at the big picture and strategic direction of the organization. They are more concerned with innovation and change.
   - **Culture and Values:** Leaders help shape the organizational culture and values by embodying and promoting them. They set the tone for ethical behavior and shared values.

- **People-Centric:** Leaders prioritize the development and growth of their team members. They empower individuals, encourage creativity, and build strong, loyal relationships.
- **Risk-Taking:** Leaders are often more willing to take calculated risks and embrace change as they seek to lead the organization to new heights.

2. **Management:**
   - **Planning and Organization:** Management is about planning, organizing, and controlling resources and processes to achieve specific objectives. Managers focus on the "how" and "when."
   - **Authority and Control:** Managers have formal authority and responsibility for making decisions and ensuring that tasks are completed as efficiently as possible.
   - **Short-Term Focus:** Managers typically operate with a short-term perspective, concentrating on day-to-day operations, efficiency, and achieving immediate goals.
   - **Rules and Procedures:** Managers establish and enforce rules, procedures, and policies to maintain order and consistency in the organization.
   - **Task-Oriented:** Managers are more concerned with ensuring that tasks are accomplished and may not always prioritize individual development or team morale.
   - **Risk-Averse:** Managers tend to be risk-averse, as they seek to maintain stability and control within the organization.

In practice, the most effective leaders often possess strong management skills, and successful managers can also exhibit leadership qualities. The key is finding a balance between the two roles, especially in positions of authority. Here are some key takeaways:

- Effective leaders inspire and set a vision, while managers plan and execute.
- A good leader motivates and empowers their team, while a manager ensures tasks are carried out efficiently.
- The best leaders understand when to manage and when to lead, and they adapt their approach accordingly.
- Leadership and management complement each other, and both are essential for a well-functioning organization.

Successful organizations benefit from a blend of strong leadership and effective management, with each role contributing its unique strengths to achieve the company's goals.

8.3 Team Culture

Team culture, also known as organizational culture or corporate culture, refers to the shared values, beliefs, behaviors, and norms that shape the identity and character of a group of individuals working together in an organization or on a specific project. A healthy and positive team culture is crucial for fostering collaboration, motivation, and overall success. Here's how to cultivate and maintain a positive team culture:

1. **Define Core Values:** Start by identifying the core values and principles that your team or organization wants to uphold. These values should align with the company's mission and vision.
2. **Lead by Example:** Leaders and team managers should exemplify the desired values and behaviors. Their actions set the tone for the team's culture.
3. **Open Communication:** Encourage open and transparent communication. Ensure that team members feel comfortable sharing their ideas, concerns, and feedback.
4. **Collaboration:** Promote collaboration and teamwork. Encourage team members to work together, share knowledge, and support each other in achieving common goals.
5. **Respect and Inclusivity:** Foster an environment of respect, inclusivity, and diversity. Ensure that all team members feel valued and respected, regardless of their background or differences.
6. **Recognition and Appreciation:** Recognize and appreciate the efforts and achievements of team members. Regularly acknowledge their contributions to boost morale and motivation.
7. **Professional Development:** Support the professional growth of team members by providing opportunities for training, skill development, and advancement within the organization.
8. **Empowerment:** Empower team members to take ownership of their work. Allow them to make decisions within their scope and encourage them to take initiative.
9. **Accountability:** Hold team members accountable for their responsibilities and commitments. Ensure that there are clear expectations and consequences for actions.

10. **Adaptability:** Be open to change and adaptability. A culture that embraces change and innovation is more likely to thrive in a dynamic business environment.
11. **Work-Life Balance:** Promote a healthy work-life balance. Encourage team members to prioritize their well-being and manage stress effectively.
12. **Celebrating Achievements:** Celebrate both small and significant achievements, milestones, and successes. This can boost team morale and create a sense of accomplishment.
13. **Conflict Resolution:** Develop effective conflict resolution mechanisms to address issues and disagreements in a constructive manner. Conflict should be seen as an opportunity for growth and improvement.
14. **Feedback Mechanisms:** Establish clear feedback channels for team members to provide input and receive feedback on their performance and the team's dynamics.
15. **Continuous Improvement:** Encourage a culture of continuous improvement. Teams should always seek to enhance their processes, products, and services.
16. **Regular Team Building:** Organize team-building activities to strengthen relationships and trust among team members.
17. **Consistency:** Ensure that the team culture remains consistent across the organization. All team leaders and members should align with the defined values and principles.

Team culture is an ongoing effort that requires commitment and consistency. It plays a significant role in the overall success and satisfaction of your team members, so investing time and effort into nurturing a positive team culture is well worth it.

8.4 Outsourcing and Freelancers

Outsourcing and hiring freelancers are two popular strategies that businesses use to access specialized skills, reduce costs, and increase flexibility. Both approaches involve contracting individuals or external organizations to perform specific tasks or projects. Here's an overview of outsourcing and hiring freelancers, along with their advantages and considerations:

1. **Outsourcing:**

- What Is It? Outsourcing involves contracting external companies or service providers to perform specific business functions or processes, often on a long-term basis. Common areas for outsourcing include customer support, IT services, manufacturing, and human resources.

a. **Advantages:**
  - Access to specialized expertise.
  - Cost savings due to lower labor costs and economies of scale.
  - Focus on core business activities.
  - Scalability and flexibility to meet changing demands.
  - Reduced administrative burden.

b. **Considerations:**
  - Loss of direct control over processes and employees.
  - Potential communication and cultural challenges with offshore outsourcing.
  - The need for a robust contract and service-level agreements (SLAs) to protect your interests.
  - Confidentiality and data security concerns.

2. **Hiring Freelancers:**
  - What Is It? Freelancers are independent professionals who provide services on a project basis. They work remotely or on-site and can be hired for tasks ranging from content writing and graphic design to software development and consulting.

a. **Advantages:**
  - Access to a global pool of talent.
  - Flexible engagement for short-term or one-off projects.
  - Reduced overhead costs, as you don't need to provide office space or benefits.
  - Speedy recruitment, as you can find freelancers quickly.
  - Pay for specific deliverables or hours worked.

b. **Considerations:**
  - Less control over the freelancer's work hours and methods.
  - Potential challenges in managing remote workers.
  - Varying quality and reliability among freelancers.
  - Intellectual property and data security concerns.
  - Legal and tax considerations in hiring independent contractors.

When deciding between outsourcing and hiring freelancers, consider the nature of the work, the level of control you need, the budget, and the timeframe for the project. In some cases, a combination of both approaches may be the most suitable option.

Here are some key tips for successful outsourcing and hiring freelancers:

- **Clearly Define the Scope:** Provide a detailed project scope, goals, and expectations to ensure both parties have a shared understanding.
- **Set Clear Communication Channels:** Establish effective communication methods and frequency to keep everyone aligned.
- **Screen and Select Carefully:** When hiring freelancers, evaluate their qualifications, portfolio, and reviews to choose the most suitable candidates.
- **Use Contracts and Agreements:** Create clear contracts or agreements outlining project details, payment terms, deliverables, and timelines.
- **Manage and Monitor Progress:** Stay involved in the process, regularly checking the work, and addressing any issues promptly.
- **Protect Your Data:** Implement security measures to safeguard your sensitive data and intellectual property.
- **Feedback and Reviews:** Provide constructive feedback and consider leaving reviews to help build a freelancer's reputation and improve future collaborations.

Both outsourcing and freelancers offer opportunities to leverage external expertise and resources to advance your business goals, but successful outcomes depend on effective planning, communication, and management.

O perations and logistics are key components of the supply chain and business management that play a crucial role in ensuring the smooth and efficient functioning of an organization. Here's an overview of these concepts:

1. **Operations:**
a. **Definition:** Operations refer to the day-to-day activities and processes that a business undertakes to produce goods and services.
b. **Key Aspects:**
   - **Production:** This involves the manufacturing or creation of products or services. It includes processes, quality control, and technology.
   - **Inventory Management:** Managing stock levels and ensuring products are available when needed while minimizing holding costs.
   - **Resource Allocation:** Allocating resources like labor, materials, and equipment efficiently to meet demand.
   - **Quality Control:** Ensuring products meet quality standards and are defect-free.
   - **Cost Management:** Managing costs to optimize profitability.
   - **Process Improvement:** Continuously improving processes to increase efficiency and reduce waste.

- **Goals:** Efficient operations aim to meet customer demand with high-quality products at the lowest possible cost.

2. **Logistics:**

a. **Definition:** Logistics involve the planning, execution, and management of the flow of goods and services, information, and resources from the point of origin to the point of consumption.

b. **Key Aspects:**
   - **Transportation:** Selecting the most suitable mode of transport (e.g., truck, ship, air, rail) to move goods from suppliers to customers.
   - **Warehousing:** Managing storage facilities for goods and optimizing their distribution.
   - **Inventory Management:** Maintaining adequate inventory levels to meet demand while avoiding overstock or stockouts.
   - **Information Flow:** Managing information about the movement of goods, inventory, and order status.
   - **Supply Chain Coordination:** Collaborating with suppliers, manufacturers, and customers to ensure efficient operations.
   - **Risk Management:** Dealing with potential disruptions in the supply chain (e.g., natural disasters, political instability).
   - **Goals:** Efficient logistics aim to reduce lead times, minimize transportation costs, and improve customer satisfaction.

3. **Integration of Operations and Logistics:**
   - Seamless coordination between operations and logistics is essential for overall supply chain efficiency.
   - Effective communication and data sharing between these functions enable better decision-making and improved customer service.
   - Technologies like Enterprise Resource Planning (ERP) systems and supply chain management software help integrate and streamline both operations and logistics.

In summary, operations focus on the internal processes of producing goods and services, while logistics deal with the movement and management of those products across the supply chain. Together, they ensure that a company can meet customer demand efficiently, minimize costs, and maintain a competitive edge in the market.

9.1 Setting Up Business Operations

Setting up business operations involves a series of crucial steps to ensure your company functions efficiently and effectively. Here is a guide on how to set up business operations:

1. **Business Plan:**
   - Start with a comprehensive business plan that outlines your business goals, mission, and vision. This plan should also include your market analysis, target audience, and financial projections.
2. **Legal Structure:**
   - Choose a legal structure for your business, such as a sole proprietorship, partnership, LLC, or corporation. This decision will impact taxation, liability, and operational requirements.
3. **Business Registration and Compliance:**
   - Register your business with the appropriate government authorities and obtain any necessary licenses and permits. Ensure you comply with local, state, and federal regulations.
4. **Location and Facilities:**
   - Secure a suitable location for your business, whether it's a physical storefront, office space, or an online platform. Consider factors like accessibility, cost, and proximity to suppliers and customers.
5. **Finances:**
   - Set up a business bank account to separate personal and business finances. Create a financial plan, secure initial funding, and establish a system for financial management, including accounting software and procedures.
6. **Supply Chain and Procurement:**
   - Identify and establish relationships with suppliers and vendors. Negotiate terms, such as pricing, delivery, and payment schedules, to ensure a smooth supply chain.
7. **Staffing:**
   - Hire and train employees as needed. Develop job descriptions, create an organizational structure, and establish HR processes, including payroll, benefits, and compliance with labor laws.
8. **Technology and Equipment:**

- Invest in the necessary technology, equipment, and tools to support your operations. This may include computers, software, machinery, and communication systems.

9. **Inventory Management:**
   - If you're dealing with physical products, implement a system for inventory management to track stock levels, reorder points, and reduce waste.

10. **Quality Control:**
    - Develop quality control processes to ensure your products or services meet or exceed customer expectations. Implement testing and inspection procedures as needed.

11. **Marketing and Sales:**
    - Create a marketing strategy to promote your business. Develop sales processes and train your team on sales techniques and customer relationship management.

12. **Customer Service:**
    - Establish a customer service department or process to handle inquiries, complaints, and support for your customers. Focus on providing excellent customer experiences.

13. **Information Technology (IT) and Data Security:**
    - Set up IT infrastructure, cybersecurity measures, and data management protocols to protect your business data and customer information.

14. **Legal and Contracts:**
    - Create or review legal contracts, such as employee contracts, vendor agreements, and customer terms and conditions. Consult with legal professionals as needed.

15. **Risk Management:**
    - Identify potential risks to your business and develop risk management strategies. Consider insurance coverage, emergency plans, and contingency measures.

16. **Sustainability and Environmental Considerations:**
    - Incorporate sustainable practices into your operations, reducing your environmental impact and appealing to eco-conscious customers.

17. **Documentation and Standard Operating Procedures (SOPs):**

- Document all key processes and create SOPs. This will help streamline operations, ensure consistency, and facilitate training of new employees.

18. **Testing and Adjustments:**
    - Before a full-scale launch, conduct tests and pilot runs to identify and resolve any operational issues.

19. **Scaling and Growth Plans:**
    - Develop plans for scaling your operations as your business grows, including strategies for expansion, new products or services, and additional locations.

20. **Continuous Improvement:**
    - Regularly assess and improve your operations to enhance efficiency, reduce costs, and adapt to changing market conditions.

Setting up business operations is a complex and ongoing process that requires careful planning and attention to detail. It's crucial to be adaptable and responsive to changing circumstances to ensure long-term success. Consider seeking advice from business experts, mentors, and consultants as you embark on this journey.

9.2 Supply Chain Management

Supply Chain Management (SCM) is a critical component of business operations that involves the planning, control, and optimization of the flow of goods, information, and finances as they move from the supplier to the manufacturer, wholesaler, retailer, and ultimately to the end consumer. SCM plays a vital role in ensuring the efficiency and effectiveness of the entire supply chain, from procurement to distribution. Here are the key aspects of supply chain management:

1. **Procurement:** This involves sourcing raw materials, components, and goods from suppliers. It includes supplier selection, negotiation, and the establishment of contracts or agreements.
2. **Production:** Managing the manufacturing and assembly processes to transform raw materials into finished products efficiently and cost-effectively. This includes optimizing production schedules, quality control, and capacity planning.
3. **Inventory Management:** Balancing the need to have products readily available to meet demand while minimizing holding costs.

Effective inventory management ensures products are in the right place at the right time.

4. **Logistics and Transportation:** Selecting the most suitable transportation methods (e.g., truck, ship, air, rail) for moving goods within the supply chain. Managing distribution centers, warehouses, and fulfillment operations is also crucial.

5. **Demand Planning and Forecasting:** Predicting future demand for products and services to ensure the supply chain can meet customer expectations while minimizing excess inventory.

6. **Information Flow:** Efficiently managing the flow of information across the supply chain, including real-time data on inventory levels, orders, shipments, and demand. This enables timely decision-making and coordination.

7. **Supplier Relationship Management (SRM):** Building and maintaining strong relationships with suppliers to ensure a reliable supply of materials, components, and goods. SRM involves communication, collaboration, and performance measurement.

8. **Risk Management:** Identifying and mitigating potential risks in the supply chain, such as natural disasters, political instability, and disruptions in the transportation network.

9. **Sustainability and Environmental Considerations:** Implementing eco-friendly practices in supply chain operations to reduce the environmental impact, improve sustainability, and meet regulatory requirements.

10. **Collaboration and Integration:** Collaborating with various partners in the supply chain, such as suppliers, manufacturers, distributors, and retailers, to streamline operations and optimize efficiency.

11. **Technology and Software:** Implementing supply chain management software (e.g., Enterprise Resource Planning or ERP systems) to automate and streamline various processes, improve data accuracy, and enable real-time visibility.

12. **Performance Measurement and KPIs:** Establishing key performance indicators (KPIs) to assess the effectiveness and efficiency of supply chain operations. This includes metrics related to cost, quality, lead times, and customer service.

13. **Continuous Improvement:** Regularly evaluating and improving supply chain processes and strategies to adapt to changing market conditions, reduce costs, and enhance customer satisfaction.

Effective supply chain management helps businesses achieve several benefits, including cost reduction, increased customer satisfaction, shorter lead times, better inventory control, and improved overall operational efficiency. It's a dynamic field that constantly evolves with technological advancements, market shifts, and global factors, and it plays a crucial role in a company's competitiveness and success in today's global economy.

9.3 Inventory Control

Inventory control, also known as inventory management, is a critical aspect of supply chain management and business operations. It involves the planning, organization, and supervision of an organization's inventory of goods, raw materials, components, and finished products. The primary goal of inventory control is to strike a balance between having enough inventory on hand to meet customer demand and avoiding excess inventory, which can lead to increased holding costs and obsolescence. Here are key components and best practices of inventory control:

1. **Inventory Classification:**
   - Categorize inventory items based on factors like demand, value, and criticality. Common classifications include ABC analysis, where "A" items are high-value and "C" items are low-value with lower demand.
2. **Reorder Point and Safety Stock:**
   - Determine reorder points for each item, which trigger a replenishment order when inventory levels reach a certain threshold. Safety stock is an extra quantity kept on hand to account for unexpected fluctuations in demand or lead times.
3. **Lead Time Management:**
   - Monitor and manage lead times, which are the time intervals between placing an order and receiving the inventory. Reducing lead times can help minimize safety stock requirements.
4. **Demand Forecasting:**
   - Use historical data and demand forecasting techniques to predict future demand accurately. This information helps in setting inventory levels and reorder points.
5. **Just-In-Time (JIT) Inventory:**

- Implement JIT inventory systems to reduce carrying costs by ordering and receiving inventory only when it's needed for production or customer demand.

6. **Economic Order Quantity (EOQ):**
   - Calculate the optimal order quantity that minimizes total inventory costs by balancing order costs and holding costs. The EOQ formula helps in finding this balance.

7. **Inventory Valuation:**
   - Keep track of the value of inventory for financial reporting purposes. Common valuation methods include FIFO (First-In-First-Out), LIFO (Last-In-First-Out), and weighted average cost.

8. **Cycle Counting:**
   - Regularly count and reconcile small subsets of inventory items in cycles rather than conducting a full physical inventory count. This helps identify discrepancies and correct them quickly.

9. **Supplier Collaboration:**
   - Work closely with suppliers to establish accurate lead times and maintain a reliable supply chain. Collaborative relationships can reduce the risk of stockouts and excess inventory.

10. **Inventory Software:**
    - Utilize inventory management software and systems to automate and streamline processes, track inventory levels in real time, and generate reports for better decision-making.

11. **Stock Rotation and Shelf Life Management:**
    - Prioritize older inventory to reduce the risk of obsolescence. Use the first-in-first-out (FIFO) method to ensure older stock is used before newer stock.

12. **ABC Analysis:**
    - Apply the Pareto principle, which suggests that roughly 20% of items are responsible for 80% of inventory value. This principle can help focus resources on managing the most critical items effectively.

13. **Performance Metrics:**

    - Establish key performance indicators (KPIs) to measure the effectiveness of inventory control, such as inventory turnover, carrying cost, and service level.

14. Continuous Improvement:
- Regularly review and update inventory control policies and practices to adapt to changes in demand, market conditions, and industry trends.

Efficient inventory control not only helps businesses reduce holding costs and improve cash flow but also ensures that customers receive products when they need them. It's a critical element in supply chain management, and the right strategies can contribute significantly to a company's profitability and customer satisfaction.

9.4 Quality Assurance

Quality assurance (QA) is a systematic approach to ensuring that products or services meet or exceed established quality standards and expectations. It is a critical part of business operations and plays a vital role in customer satisfaction, product safety, and regulatory compliance. Here are the key components and best practices of quality assurance:

1. **Quality Standards and Criteria:**
   - Define clear and measurable quality standards and criteria that products or services must meet. These standards can be based on industry best practices, regulatory requirements, or customer expectations.
2. **Quality Control Processes:**
   - Implement processes and procedures to monitor, inspect, and test products or services at various stages of production or delivery. This includes incoming inspections, in-process checks, and final product evaluations.
3. **Documented Quality Policies:**
   - Create documented quality policies and procedures that outline how quality is assured throughout the organization. These documents serve as a reference for employees and can be used for training.
4. **Training and Education:**
   - Train employees at all levels to understand and implement quality standards and procedures. Continuous education and training programs help ensure that employees are up-to-date with the latest quality practices.
5. **Supplier Quality Assurance:**

- Collaborate with suppliers to ensure they provide high-quality materials, components, or services. Implement supplier quality assurance processes to assess and monitor their performance.

6. **Root Cause Analysis:**
   - When defects or issues arise, conduct root cause analysis to identify the underlying reasons for the problem. Addressing root causes helps prevent similar issues in the future.

7. **Quality Audits:**
   - Conduct regular internal audits to evaluate adherence to quality standards and identify areas for improvement. External audits by third-party organizations may also be necessary for certain industries.

8. **Statistical Process Control (SPC):**
   - Use statistical techniques to monitor and control production processes. This helps in identifying variations and ensuring that processes are consistent and in control.

9. **Continuous Improvement:**
   - Promote a culture of continuous improvement, often through methodologies like Six Sigma or Total Quality Management (TQM). These approaches focus on process improvement and waste reduction.

10. **Quality Metrics and KPIs:**
    - Define and measure key performance indicators (KPIs) related to quality, such as defect rates, customer complaints, and on-time delivery. These metrics help in tracking and managing quality.

11. **Customer Feedback and Satisfaction:**
    - Regularly collect and analyze customer feedback to understand their satisfaction levels and identify areas for improvement. Address customer complaints and concerns promptly.

12. **Regulatory Compliance:**
    - Ensure that your products or services comply with industry-specific regulations and standards. Keep updated on any changes in regulations and make necessary adjustments to processes.

13. **Quality Certifications:**
    - Obtain relevant quality certifications, such as ISO 9001, to demonstrate a commitment to quality and enhance the organization's reputation.

14. Risk Management:
- Identify and manage risks related to quality that could affect the business, reputation, or safety of customers. Develop contingency plans for mitigating quality-related risks.

15. Transparency and Communication:
- Foster open communication within the organization to encourage reporting of quality issues and ensure that employees at all levels understand the importance of quality assurance.

Quality assurance is not a one-time activity but an ongoing process that involves all aspects of a business. It is essential for building trust with customers, reducing waste, and maintaining a competitive edge in the market. By consistently delivering high-quality products or services, businesses can enhance their reputation and customer loyalty.

Managing your finances is a critical aspect of personal and financial well-being. Proper financial management can help you achieve your goals, whether it's saving for retirement, buying a home, paying off debt, or simply living a comfortable life. Here are some key steps and principles to consider when managing your finances:

1. **Create a Budget:**
   - Start by tracking your income and expenses. A budget helps you understand where your money is coming from and where it's going. There are many budgeting apps and tools available to assist with this.
2. **Set Financial Goals:**
   - Define short-term and long-term financial goals, such as saving for a vacation, buying a home, or building an emergency fund. Having clear goals will help you stay motivated and focused.
3. **Emergency Fund:**
   - Build an emergency fund that can cover three to six months' worth of living expenses. This fund can help you weather unexpected financial crises without going into debt.
4. **Debt Management:**

- If you have high-interest debt (like credit card debt), make a plan to pay it off as quickly as possible. Use strategies like the debt snowball or debt avalanche to tackle your debts.

5. **Savings and Investments:**
   - Save a portion of your income regularly. Consider investing your savings in assets like stocks, bonds, and real estate to help your money grow over time. Diversify your investments to manage risk.

6. **Retirement Planning:**
   - Start saving for retirement as early as possible. Contribute to retirement accounts such as 401(k)s, IRAs, or other government-sponsored plans. Take advantage of employer matching if available.

7. **Insurance:**
   - Ensure you have appropriate insurance coverage, including health, life, disability, and home or renter's insurance. Insurance can protect you from unexpected expenses and risks.

8. **Live Below Your Means:**
   - Avoid lifestyle inflation by spending less than you earn. This provides room for savings and helps you build wealth over time.

9. **Regularly Review and Adjust:**
   - Periodically review your budget and financial goals. Adjust your plan as needed based on changes in your income, expenses, and goals.

10. **Seek Professional Advice:**
    - If you're unsure about your financial situation, consider seeking advice from a financial advisor or planner. They can provide tailored guidance based on your circumstances.

11. **Tax Planning:**
    - Understand your tax obligations and look for opportunities to minimize your tax liability legally. This might include taking advantage of tax-advantaged accounts or tax deductions.

12. **Mindful Spending:**
    - Be mindful of your spending habits and distinguish between wants and needs. Cut unnecessary expenses and allocate more funds to your financial goals.

13. **Automate Finances:**

- Set up automatic transfers to your savings and investment accounts. This ensures you consistently save and invest without needing to think about it.

14. Build and Maintain Good Credit:
- A good credit score can help you secure loans at favorable interest rates. Pay your bills on time, manage credit responsibly, and periodically check your credit report for errors.

15. Stay Informed:
- Stay up-to-date on financial news and trends. Understanding the broader economic picture can help you make informed decisions about your investments and financial strategies.

Remember that managing finances is a continuous process. It requires discipline, patience, and a long-term perspective. By following these principles and regularly assessing and adjusting your financial plan, you can work toward financial stability and reach your financial goals.

10.1 Financial Management Basics

Financial management basics are fundamental principles and practices that help individuals and organizations effectively handle their finances. Whether you're managing personal finances or overseeing a business's financial health, these basics are essential for making informed decisions and achieving financial stability. Here are the key financial management basics:

1. **Budgeting:**
   - Create a budget to track income and expenses. A budget helps you allocate funds for different purposes and ensures you live within your means.
2. **Financial Goals:**
   - Set clear financial goals, both short-term and long-term. These goals provide a roadmap for your financial decisions and help you stay focused.
3. **Emergency Fund:**
   - Build an emergency fund with at least three to six months' worth of living expenses. This fund acts as a financial safety net in case of unexpected events, such as medical emergencies or job loss.
4. **Debt Management:**

- Manage and reduce high-interest debts, such as credit card debt, through strategies like debt consolidation, the debt snowball, or the debt avalanche method.

5. **Savings:**
   - Save a portion of your income regularly. Consider creating separate savings accounts for specific goals, such as an emergency fund, vacation, or a down payment on a home.

6. **Investing:**
   - Invest your savings in assets like stocks, bonds, mutual funds, and real estate. Diversify your investments to spread risk and achieve potential growth over time.

7. **Retirement Planning:**
   - Start saving for retirement early in your career. Contribute to retirement accounts like 401(k)s or IRAs, and take advantage of employer matching contributions if available.

8. **Insurance:**
   - Ensure you have appropriate insurance coverage for your needs, including health, life, disability, and property insurance. Insurance protects you from unexpected financial risks.

9. **Living Within Your Means:**
   - Avoid spending more than you earn. Living below your means allows you to save and invest for the future.

10. **Regular Review and Adjustment:**
    - Periodically review your financial situation and adjust your budget and goals as needed. Life circumstances change, so your financial plan should be flexible.

11. **Tax Planning:**
    - Understand tax laws and explore opportunities to minimize your tax liability legally. Utilize tax-advantaged accounts and take advantage of tax deductions.

12. **Professional Advice:**
    - If you're unsure about your financial situation, consider consulting a financial advisor or planner for personalized guidance.

13. **Credit Management:**
    - Maintain a good credit score by paying bills on time and managing credit responsibly. A good credit score can help you secure loans at favorable terms.

14. Automate Finances:
- Set up automatic transfers for savings and investments to ensure you consistently work toward your financial goals.

15. Financial Education:
- Continuously educate yourself about personal finance and investment principles. Staying informed about financial news and trends can help you make informed decisions.

These financial management basics are applicable to individuals and businesses alike. By following these principles, you can make sound financial decisions, achieve your goals, and build a strong financial foundation for the future.

10.2 Budgeting and Forecasting

Budgeting and forecasting are essential financial management processes used by individuals, businesses, and organizations to plan and control their finances. While they are related concepts, they serve different purposes:

1. Budgeting:

Budgeting is the process of creating a detailed financial plan that outlines expected income and expenses over a specific period, typically a month, quarter, or year. The primary goals of budgeting are to:

- **Control Spending:** A budget helps you allocate resources to various categories (e.g., housing, groceries, entertainment) and ensures that your spending aligns with your financial goals.
- **Set Financial Goals:** Budgets allow you to allocate funds to specific financial objectives, such as saving for a vacation, paying off debt, or building an emergency fund.
- **Track Performance:** By comparing actual income and expenses to the budget, you can assess your financial performance and make necessary adjustments.

The basic steps in personal budgeting include:

- Identify your sources of income.
- List your monthly expenses, categorizing them as fixed (e.g., rent, mortgage) or variable (e.g., groceries, entertainment).
- Create a budget that balances income and expenses.

- Monitor and track your actual spending against the budget.

2. Business Budgeting:

In a business context, budgeting is more complex and may involve different types of budgets, such as the operating budget (revenue and expenses), capital budget (long-term investments), and cash flow budget (cash inflows and outflows). Business budgets help plan for growth, allocate resources, and ensure financial stability.

3. Forecasting:

Forecasting is a financial planning process that involves making predictions about future financial performance based on historical data and assumptions. The primary goals of forecasting are to:

- **Anticipate Future Trends:** Forecasting allows you to predict future financial trends, such as sales growth, market demand, or revenue projections.
- **Make Informed Decisions:** Forecasts provide valuable insights for decision-making, whether it's expanding a business, adjusting pricing strategies, or planning for contingencies.
- **Allocate Resources:** Organizations use forecasts to allocate resources efficiently, such as deciding how much inventory to order or how many employees to hire.

There are different methods for forecasting, such as time series analysis, regression analysis, and market research. In business, financial forecasting often involves preparing financial statements (income statements, balance sheets, and cash flow statements) for future periods.

Key steps in the budgeting and forecasting process include:

- **Gather Data:** Collect historical financial data, market research, and relevant information.
- **Set Assumptions:** Define the assumptions that will drive your budget or forecast. These might include inflation rates, interest rates, sales growth, and cost projections.
- **Create Projections:** Develop a financial plan based on your assumptions. For budgeting, this means allocating resources to specific categories. For forecasting, it involves projecting future financial statements.

- **Review and Adjust:** Continuously review and adjust your budget or forecast as conditions change. Flexibility and adaptability are critical.

Budgeting and forecasting are essential tools for managing finances and making informed financial decisions, whether you are an individual, business owner, or financial manager. These processes help you set and achieve financial goals while planning for the future.

4. Cash Flow Management

Cash flow management is a crucial aspect of financial management for individuals and businesses. It involves monitoring, analyzing, and optimizing the flow of cash into and out of your accounts to ensure you have enough liquidity to meet your financial obligations and take advantage of opportunities. Effective cash flow management is essential for maintaining financial stability and achieving your financial goals. Here are some key principles and strategies for managing cash flow:

a. **For Individuals:**
- **Budgeting:** Create a personal budget to track your income and expenses. This helps you understand where your money is going and identify areas where you can reduce expenses.
- **Emergency Fund:** Maintain an emergency fund with at least three to six months' worth of living expenses. This fund serves as a financial safety net for unexpected events.
- **Regular Monitoring:** Keep a close eye on your bank and credit card statements to identify any discrepancies or unauthorized transactions. This helps prevent fraud and ensures you're aware of your spending patterns.
- **Automate Savings:** Set up automatic transfers to your savings and investment accounts. Automating your savings ensures that you consistently save and invest.
- **Reduce Debt:** Pay off high-interest debts as quickly as possible. Reducing debt not only frees up cash flow but also reduces interest expenses.
- **Emergency Expenses:** Be prepared for unexpected expenses, such as medical bills or car repairs, by having a separate fund or credit available to cover these costs.

- **Increase Income:** Look for opportunities to increase your income, such as side jobs, freelancing, or passive income streams like investments.

b. **For Businesses:**
- **Cash Flow Statement:** Create and regularly update a cash flow statement, which tracks cash inflows and outflows. This helps you understand the timing of your cash transactions.
- **Accounts Receivable Management:** Ensure that you have an efficient accounts receivable process to collect payments from customers on time. Offer discounts for early payments and establish clear credit policies.
- **Accounts Payable Management**: Manage your accounts payable carefully, negotiating favorable terms with suppliers and taking advantage of discounts for early payments.
- **Working Capital Management:** Maintain an optimal level of working capital, which is the difference between current assets and current liabilities. This ensures you have enough liquidity for daily operations.
- **Inventory Control:** Manage your inventory levels efficiently to avoid tying up excessive cash in unsold products.
- **Emergency Reserves:** Just as individuals have emergency funds, businesses should have reserves to cover unexpected expenses or disruptions in operations.
- **Forecasting:** Regularly update cash flow forecasts to anticipate cash needs and potential surpluses. This helps in proactive decision-making.
- **Access to Credit:** Establish lines of credit or short-term loans to cover cash flow gaps during slow periods.
- **Cost Control:** Continuously review and control operating expenses to free up cash.
- **Revenue Diversification:** Look for ways to diversify your revenue streams to reduce dependency on a single source.

Effective cash flow management involves balancing your cash inflows and outflows to maintain liquidity and financial stability. Regularly review and update your cash flow plan, adjust your strategies as needed, and be prepared for unexpected financial challenges. Whether you're an individual or a business owner, sound cash flow management is a key component of financial success.

Tax planning is the process of managing your financial affairs in a way that reduces your tax liability while remaining compliant with tax laws. Effective tax planning allows individuals and businesses to legally minimize their tax obligations, keeping more of their hard-earned money. Here are some essential tax planning strategies:

1. **For Individuals:**

Understand Your Tax Situation: Familiarize yourself with the tax laws and regulations that apply to your specific situation, including federal, state, and local taxes. Know your tax brackets, deductions, and credits.

a. **Maximize Tax-Efficient Accounts:** Contribute to tax-advantaged accounts such as 401(k)s, IRAs, and Health Savings Accounts (HSAs). These accounts can reduce your taxable income and help you save for retirement or medical expenses.

b. **Take Advantage of Tax Deductions and Credits:**
   - Identify deductions and credits you qualify for, such as the Earned Income Tax Credit (EITC), the Child Tax Credit, and the mortgage interest deduction.
   - Consider itemizing deductions if it results in a lower tax liability than taking the standard deduction.

c. **Invest Tax-Efficiently:**
   - Invest in tax-efficient funds or assets, such as index funds, which typically generate fewer capital gains.
   - Use tax-loss harvesting to offset capital gains with capital losses.

d. **Strategic Timing:** Be mindful of the timing of income and expenses. For example, you can defer income into the following tax year or accelerate deductions in the current year to reduce your taxable income.

e. **Consider Roth Accounts:** Roth IRAs and Roth 401(k)s allow for tax-free withdrawals in retirement. Consider converting traditional retirement accounts to Roth accounts if it's beneficial in your situation.

f. Gift and Inheritance Planning: Understand the gift tax and estate tax rules to minimize the tax impact when transferring assets to heirs. Use the annual gift tax exclusion and lifetime estate tax exemption effectively.

g. **Education Planning:** Take advantage of tax-advantaged education savings accounts like 529 plans to save for future education expenses.

h. **Charitable Giving:** Contribute to qualified charities to deduct donations from your taxable income. Consider donating appreciated assets for additional tax benefits.

2. **For Businesses:**

a. **Choose the Right Business Structure:** Select a business entity (e.g., sole proprietorship, LLC, S corporation, C corporation) that aligns with your tax planning goals.

b. **Tax Credits:** Identify and take advantage of business tax credits, such as the Research and Development (R&D) tax credit and the Small Business Health Care Tax Credit.

c. **Expense Deductions:** Maximize deductions for business expenses, including operating costs, travel expenses, and employee benefits.

d. **Depreciation and Amortization:** Use depreciation and amortization deductions to recover the cost of capital assets over time.

e. **Hire Tax Credits:** If you hire certain groups of individuals, you may qualify for federal and state employment-related tax credits.

f. **Retirement Plans:** Offer retirement plans for employees, such as 401(k) plans, which can provide tax benefits and attract talent.

g. **Health Benefits:** Provide tax-advantaged health benefits to employees through Health Savings Accounts (HSAs) and Flexible Spending Accounts (FSAs).

h. **State and Local Taxes:** Be aware of state and local tax laws, as they can vary significantly and impact your tax liability.

i. **Keep Accurate Records:** Maintain meticulous financial records and documentation to support deductions and credits.

j. **Consult Tax Professionals:** Seek guidance from tax professionals, such as CPAs or tax advisors, who can provide personalized advice and help you navigate complex tax regulations.

Effective tax planning requires careful consideration of your specific financial situation and goals. It's essential to remain compliant with tax laws while exploring opportunities to reduce your tax burden. Consulting with a qualified tax professional can be valuable in creating a tax strategy that is both legal and beneficial for your financial well-being.

10.4 Financial Reporting

Financial reporting is the process of creating and distributing financial statements and other reports that provide an accurate and comprehensive view of an entity's financial performance and position. Financial reporting is crucial for various stakeholders, including investors, creditors, management, and government agencies, to assess an entity's financial health and make informed decisions. Here are the key components and principles of financial reporting:

1. **Components of Financial Reporting:**
   - **Financial Statements:** The core of financial reporting consists of several key financial statements:
   - **Balance Sheet (or Statement of Financial Position):** Provides an overview of an entity's assets, liabilities, and equity at a specific point in time.
   - **Income Statement (or Profit and Loss Statement):** Summarizes an entity's revenues, expenses, and net income (or loss) over a specific period.
   - **Cash Flow Statement:** Shows the inflow and outflow of cash and cash equivalents during a given period, categorizing them into operating, investing, and financing activities.
   - **Statement of Changes in Equity:** Explains the changes in equity over a specified period, including contributions, distributions, and comprehensive income.
   - **Notes to the Financial Statements:** These notes provide additional context, explanations, and details related to items on the financial statements. They include information about accounting policies, contingencies, and other relevant matters.
   - **Management's Discussion and Analysis (MD&A):** Often included in annual reports, MD&A provides management's insights into the company's financial performance, significant events, and future prospects.
   - **Independent Auditor's Report:** Prepared by an external auditor, this report attests to the fairness and accuracy of the

financial statements and the entity's compliance with accounting standards.

- **Supplementary Information:** Depending on the entity's specific requirements and the interests of stakeholders, additional reports or disclosures may be included in financial reporting, such as segment reporting or earnings per share.

2. **Principles of Financial Reporting:**

- **Accuracy and Completeness:** Financial statements must be accurate, complete, and free from material misstatements or errors. Accounting standards, such as Generally Accepted Accounting Principles (GAAP) or International Financial Reporting Standards (IFRS), guide how transactions are recorded and reported.
- **Consistency:** Entities should use consistent accounting methods from one period to the next, ensuring comparability of financial information over time.
- **Relevance:** Financial reports should include information that is relevant to the needs of stakeholders. This includes disclosure of significant financial transactions, events, and conditions.
- **Transparency:** Information should be presented clearly and transparently, making it easy for stakeholders to understand the entity's financial position and performance.
- **Fair Presentation:** Financial statements should fairly represent the entity's financial status and operations. This includes presenting assets and liabilities at their fair values.
- **Materiality:** Information should be presented based on materiality, meaning that only significant items are included in the financial statements.
- **Going Concern Assumption:** Financial reports typically assume that the entity will continue its operations for the foreseeable future. If there are concerns about the entity's ability to continue as a going concern, this must be disclosed.
- **Comparability:** Financial reports should be prepared to enable users to compare an entity's financial performance and position with other periods or with other entities.
- **Regulatory Compliance:** Entities must adhere to the relevant regulatory and reporting requirements for their jurisdiction.

- **Timeliness:** Financial reports should be prepared and distributed in a timely manner, allowing stakeholders to make informed decisions based on up-to-date information.
- **Audit and Review:** External auditors may examine and report on the accuracy and reliability of an entity's financial statements. Their reports add credibility to the financial reporting process.

Financial reporting is a critical aspect of transparency and accountability in both the corporate and public sectors. It helps stakeholders make informed decisions, ensures regulatory compliance, and fosters trust in financial markets. As such, it plays a significant role in economic stability and growth.

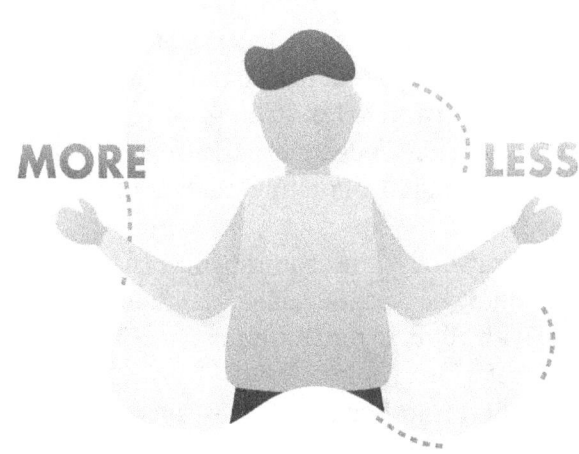

Scaling your business involves expanding its operations to accommodate more customers, increase revenue, and achieve long-term growth. It's a critical phase in a company's development, but it comes with its own set of challenges. Here are some steps to help you scale your business effectively:

1. **Evaluate Your Current State:** Before scaling, assess your business's strengths, weaknesses, and financial health. This includes understanding your current customer base, profitability, and operations.
2. **Create a Scalable Business Model:** Ensure that your business model can handle growth. Consider factors like product demand, supply chain, and staffing. Your business processes should be efficient and adaptable.
3. **Build a Strong Team:** Hiring the right talent is crucial. As you scale, you may need more employees with varied skill sets. Ensure that you have effective leadership and management in place to guide your team.
4. **Expand Your Market:** Look for opportunities to reach new customers or markets. This might involve expanding geographically or diversifying your product or service offerings.
5. **Invest in Technology:** Technology can streamline processes, improve customer experience, and help you manage the increased

workload. Invest in tools and systems that can support your scaling efforts.

6. **Secure Adequate Financing:** Scaling often requires capital investment. Whether it's through loans, investments, or reinvesting profits, make sure you have access to the necessary funds.

7. **Develop Marketing and Sales Strategies:** To attract a larger customer base, you need effective marketing and sales strategies. This could involve digital marketing, content marketing, and even partnerships.

8. **Customer Retention:** While acquiring new customers is important, don't forget about your existing ones. Maintaining a strong relationship with your current customers can lead to repeat business and referrals.

9. **Manage Cash Flow:** Scaling can put a strain on cash flow. Monitor your finances closely and manage expenses wisely to ensure you have the capital to support growth.

10. **Set Metrics and KPIs:** Establish key performance indicators (KPIs) to track your progress. This can include revenue targets, customer acquisition metrics, and operational efficiency benchmarks.

11. **Improve Operational Efficiency:** Streamline your business processes and operations to maximize productivity. Automation and lean management techniques can help.

12. **Customer Service and Quality Control:** As your business grows, maintaining high levels of customer service and product quality is essential. A reputation for reliability and quality can be a strong competitive advantage.

13. **Adapt and Iterate:** Be flexible and willing to adapt your strategy as needed. Not everything will go according to plan, and you may need to pivot or make changes to remain competitive.

14. **Risk Management:** Scaling inherently involves risks. Identify potential risks and have mitigation plans in place to deal with unexpected challenges.

15. **Legal and Compliance Issues:** As your business grows, you may face new legal and regulatory challenges. Ensure you're compliant with all relevant laws and regulations.

16. **Build a Strong Brand:** A strong brand can help you stand out in a competitive market. Invest in branding and marketing efforts to create a unique identity for your business.

Remember that scaling your business is a continuous process, and it's important to monitor your progress and adjust your strategy as necessary. It's also essential to maintain a customer-centric approach and a strong company culture throughout the scaling process to ensure long-term success.

11.1 Expanding Your Product or Service

Expanding your product or service offerings is a strategic move that can help you grow your business, reach new customers, and increase revenue. However, it should be done thoughtfully and strategically. Here's a step-by-step guide on how to effectively expand your product or service offerings:

1. **Market Research:** Begin by conducting thorough market research. Understand your target audience and their needs, as well as your competitors and the broader market trends. Identify opportunities for expansion.
2. **Customer Feedback:** Gather feedback from your existing customers. What additional products or services are they looking for? What pain points can you address with new offerings?
3. **Assess Your Capabilities:** Evaluate your internal capabilities and resources. Do you have the expertise, infrastructure, and resources to develop or offer new products or services? If not, what will you need to acquire or develop?
4. **Business Strategy:** Develop a clear business strategy for the expansion. This should include your goals, target market, pricing strategy, and marketing plan. Ensure that the new offering aligns with your overall business objectives.
5. **Product/Service Development:** If you're introducing a new product, work on its design, development, and testing. If you're expanding a service, refine your service delivery processes. Quality and reliability are paramount.
6. **Branding and Positioning:** Consider how the new offering fits within your existing brand. You may need to create a sub-brand or position the new product or service as an extension of your existing brand.
7. **Pricing Strategy:** Determine the pricing strategy for your new offering. This should consider factors like production costs, market demand, and the perceived value of the product or service.

8. **Marketing and Promotion:** Develop a marketing and promotion plan specifically tailored to the new offering. This might include a launch campaign, digital marketing, and targeted advertising.
9. **Sales Channels:** Decide how you'll sell the new product or service. Will it be sold through your existing sales channels, or do you need to establish new ones?
10. **Training and Development:** If your expansion involves offering a new service, ensure that your employees are trained and equipped to provide it at a high standard.
11. **Testing and Piloting:** Consider testing the new offering with a smaller audience or in a specific market segment before a full-scale launch. This allows you to identify and address any issues before a wider release.
12. **Feedback Loop:** Continuously gather feedback from customers and employees about the new offering. Use this information to make improvements and adjustments.
13. **Measure Success:** Establish key performance indicators (KPIs) to measure the success of the expansion. This might include sales figures, customer satisfaction ratings, and market share.
14. **Scalability:** Ensure that your operations and infrastructure can scale with the increased demand that may come with the expansion.
15. **Risk Management:** Identify potential risks and have mitigation plans in place. Expansion can be risky, so be prepared for challenges that may arise.
16. **Legal and Compliance:** Be aware of any legal and regulatory requirements that might apply to your new offering. Ensure that you are compliant with all relevant laws and regulations.
17. **Feedback and Iteration:** Be prepared to make adjustments and improvements based on the feedback and performance data. Successful expansion often involves ongoing optimization.

Expanding your product or service offerings can be a rewarding endeavor, but it should be approached with careful planning and execution. By thoroughly researching, developing a clear strategy, and continuously listening to your customers, you can increase your chances of success when expanding your offerings.

11.2 Entering New Markets

Entering new markets is a strategic move that can help your business grow and diversify its customer base. However, it requires careful planning and execution. Here are the steps to consider when entering new markets:

1. **Market Research:**
    *   Conduct in-depth market research to identify potential new markets. Look for regions or countries with demand for your products or services.
    *   Analyze the competition in these new markets. Understand their strengths and weaknesses.
    *   Evaluate the cultural, economic, and legal differences that may impact your entry.
2. **Market Segmentation:**
    *   Define your target market in the new area. Consider demographics, buying behaviors, and specific needs in the region.
    *   Develop buyer personas that represent your ideal customers in the new market.
3. **Market Entry Strategy:**
    *   Determine the most suitable market entry strategy. Options include exporting, franchising, joint ventures, partnerships, and establishing wholly-owned subsidiaries.
    *   Consider whether to start with a pilot program or a full-scale entry.
4. **Legal and Regulatory Compliance:**
    *   Understand the legal and regulatory requirements in the new market. This includes import/export regulations, licensing, intellectual property protection, and industry-specific regulations.
5. **Adapt Your Offerings:**
    *   Tailor your products or services to meet the needs and preferences of the new market. Localization may involve language, branding, packaging, or even product features.
6. **Pricing Strategy:**
    *   Develop a pricing strategy that takes into account local economic conditions, competition, and customer expectations. Consider currency exchange rates if applicable.
7. **Distribution and Supply Chain:**
    *   Establish or adapt your distribution and supply chain to efficiently reach customers in the new market.

- Build relationships with local suppliers or distributors if needed.
8. **Marketing and Promotion:**
   - Create a marketing plan that targets the new market. This should include digital marketing, advertising, and public relations strategies.
   - Consider cultural nuances in your marketing materials to avoid misunderstandings.
9. **Sales Channels:**
   - Decide on the most effective sales channels for the new market. This could include e-commerce, local partners, or a physical presence.
10. **Local Partnerships:**
    - Form partnerships with local businesses or organizations to gain market insights and build relationships with customers.
11. **Staffing and Talent:**
    - Determine if you need to hire local talent to assist with market entry. Language skills and cultural knowledge can be invaluable.
12. **Risk Assessment and Mitigation:**
    - Identify potential risks associated with entering the new market and develop risk mitigation strategies. These could include political instability, economic downturns, or legal disputes.
13. **Test and Iterate:**
    - Consider a soft launch or pilot program to test the waters and gather feedback.
    - Use the insights gained from the initial entry to make necessary adjustments.
14. **Monitoring and Evaluation:**
    - Continuously monitor the performance of your market entry efforts. Use KPIs to assess progress and success.
15. **Scale and Expand:**
    - Once you have a foothold in the new market and have validated your approach, scale up your operations as appropriate.
16. **Legal and Regulatory Compliance:**
    - Continue to stay up to date with any changes in local laws and regulations that may affect your business.

Entering new markets can be a complex process, but it can also open up significant growth opportunities for your business. Thorough research, adaptation to local conditions, and continuous evaluation will be key to your success in new markets.

13.3 Franchising and Licensing

Franchising and licensing are two business expansion strategies that allow you to extend your brand and products or services into new markets, often without the capital-intensive burden of wholly-owned expansion. However, they involve distinct legal and operational structures. Here's an overview of each approach:

1. Franchising:

a. Definition:

Franchising is a business model where a franchisor (the original business owner) grants a license to a franchisee (an independent operator) to operate a business under the franchisor's brand and within its established business framework.

b. Structure:
- Franchisors provide franchisees with a complete package that includes the brand, products or services, operational procedures, training, and ongoing support.
- Franchisees pay an upfront fee and ongoing royalties to the franchisor in exchange for using the brand and benefiting from the franchisor's systems and support.

c. Advantages:
- **Rapid expansion:** Franchising can enable fast growth, as the burden of capital investment is often on the franchisee.
- **Local knowledge:** Franchisees are typically local entrepreneurs who understand the market and customer preferences.
- **Shared risk:** Franchisees share the risk and reward of the business with the franchisor.

d. Challenges:
- **Loss of control:** Franchisors must relinquish some control to franchisees, which can lead to variations in quality and service.
- **Legal and operational complexity:** Franchising involves complex legal agreements and ongoing support and training.

e. Examples:
- McDonald's, Subway, and KFC are well-known examples of franchises.

2. **Licensing:**
a. **Definition:**

Licensing is a business arrangement where a licensor (the owner of intellectual property or a brand) grants a license to a licensee to use their intellectual property, brand, or technology under specific terms and conditions.

b. **Structure:**
   - Licenses can cover various types of intellectual property, including patents, trademarks, copyrights, and trade secrets.
   - Licensees pay royalties or fees to the licensor for the rights to use the intellectual property.
c. **Advantages:**
   - Low capital investment: Licensees typically pay fees to use the intellectual property, but they don't have to build the entire business from scratch.
   - Brand extension: Licensing allows a brand to expand into new markets and product categories without having to produce or market those products themselves.
d. **Challenges:**
   - **Quality control:** The licensor must ensure that licensees maintain the quality and standards associated with the brand or intellectual property.
   - **Legal complexities:** Licensing agreements can be legally complex, as they must define the terms and restrictions of using the intellectual property.
e. **Examples:**
   - Disney licensing its characters for merchandise, Microsoft licensing its software, and sports teams licensing their logos and brands are common examples of licensing.

Both franchising and licensing can be effective strategies for expanding your business, but the choice between them depends on your business model, the nature of your products or services, and your expansion goals. Franchising is more suitable for replicating an entire business model, while licensing is ideal for leveraging specific intellectual property or brand recognition. Each approach involves its own set of legal, operational, and financial considerations, so careful planning and legal counsel are essential.

11.4 Strategic Partnerships

Strategic partnerships are collaborative arrangements between two or more businesses to achieve common goals or objectives. These partnerships can take various forms and are often entered into to leverage each partner's strengths, resources, and expertise. Here's a guide on how to establish and benefit from strategic partnerships:

1. **Identify Objectives:**
    - Determine the specific goals and objectives you want to achieve through the partnership. It could be expanding market reach, increasing innovation, reducing costs, or accessing new technologies.
2. **Identify Potential Partners:**
    - Look for businesses or organizations that complement your goals and objectives. Consider companies in related industries or those with complementary products or services.
3. **Value Proposition:**
    - Clearly define the value you bring to the partnership. Understand what your potential partner seeks to gain and how your strengths align with their needs.
4. **Communication and Relationship Building:**
    - Initiate contact and establish a rapport with potential partners. Open and transparent communication is key in building trust.
5. **Negotiate Terms:**
    - Define the terms and specifics of the partnership in a formal agreement. This might include the scope of the partnership, responsibilities of each partner, and how resources and benefits will be shared.
6. **Legal and Regulatory Considerations:**
    - Consult legal counsel to ensure the partnership agreement is legally sound and compliant with relevant regulations and antitrust laws.
7. **Resource Sharing:**
    - Share resources such as technology, expertise, and data to achieve the partnership's objectives. This could involve co-development, shared marketing, or co-branded products.
8. **Mutual Benefit:**
    - Ensure that the partnership is mutually beneficial. Both parties should gain value and advantages from the collaboration.

9. **Performance Metrics:**
   - Establish key performance indicators (KPIs) and regular reporting mechanisms to monitor the partnership's success.
10. **Conflict Resolution:**
    - Include conflict resolution mechanisms in the agreement to address disputes or issues that may arise during the partnership.
11. **Continuous Communication:**
    - Maintain open lines of communication with your partner. Regular meetings and updates can help address issues and capitalize on opportunities.
12. **Adaptability:**
    - Be adaptable and willing to adjust the partnership as circumstances change. Businesses and markets are dynamic, and partnerships should evolve accordingly.
13. **Leverage Networks:**
    - Utilize the networks of your partners to gain access to potential clients, customers, or other business opportunities.
14. **Promotion and Marketing:**
    - Collaboratively promote the partnership and the benefits it offers to your target audience. This can enhance brand recognition and customer trust.
15. **Exit Strategy:**
    - Include provisions for ending the partnership if it no longer serves its intended purpose. This could involve a buyout, renegotiation, or a predetermined termination process.
16. **Measure and Evaluate:**
    - Continuously measure the partnership's impact on your business and its alignment with your objectives. Use this data to evaluate the partnership's effectiveness.

Strategic partnerships can be powerful tools for achieving business growth and innovation. By working with the right partners and aligning your efforts, you can leverage each other's strengths, resources, and expertise to mutual advantage. Successful partnerships require careful planning, open communication, and a commitment to the shared goals and objectives.

Handling business challenges and risks is an essential part of running any organization. To ensure the long-term success and sustainability of your business, it's crucial to have a proactive approach to identifying, managing, and mitigating these challenges and risks. Here are some steps and strategies to help you effectively handle business challenges and risks:

1. **Identify and Assess Risks:**
   - Start by identifying potential risks and challenges that your business might face. These can include financial risks, operational risks, market risks, and more.
   - Assess the probability and impact of each risk. This can be done through risk assessments and analysis, such as SWOT (Strengths, Weaknesses, Opportunities, Threats) analysis.
2. **Risk Management Strategy:**
   1. Develop a comprehensive risk management strategy that outlines how your organization plans to deal with various risks. This should include preventive measures, risk transfer mechanisms (like insurance), and contingency plans.
3. **Financial Planning:**
   2. Maintain a strong financial position with healthy cash reserves. This can act as a buffer during difficult times and help you weather financial challenges.

4. **Diversify Your Business:**
   3. Don't put all your eggs in one basket. Diversify your product or service offerings and your customer base to reduce dependency on a single source of revenue.
5. **Market Research:**
   4. Continuously conduct market research to stay informed about changing customer preferences, industry trends, and emerging risks. This information can help you adapt and stay ahead of the competition.
6. **Operational Efficiency:**
   5. Streamline your operations to reduce inefficiencies. Efficient processes are often more resilient in the face of challenges.
7. **Contingency Planning:**
   6. Develop contingency plans for potential risks, such as natural disasters, economic downturns, or cybersecurity threats. These plans should outline the steps to take if these risks materialize.
8. **Insurance:**
   7. Purchase appropriate insurance coverage for your business. This can help protect you from certain financial risks, such as property damage, liability claims, or employee-related issues.
9. **Legal and Compliance Measures:**
   8. Stay compliant with all relevant laws and regulations. Non-compliance can lead to legal issues that pose a risk to your business.
10. **Employee Training and Involvement:**
   9. Ensure your employees are aware of potential risks and know how to respond to them. Encourage a culture of risk awareness and responsible decision-making.
11. **Regular Review and Adaptation:**
   10. Regularly review your risk management strategy to ensure it remains relevant and effective. Adapt it as your business evolves and as new risks emerge.
12. **Stakeholder Communication:**

   11. Maintain open and transparent communication with stakeholders, including employees, customers, suppliers, and investors. They should be informed about potential risks and how you plan to address them.

13. Seek Professional Advice:
   12. If you're unsure about how to handle a specific risk or challenge, consider seeking advice from experts, consultants, or industry peers who may have faced similar situations.

14. Scenario Planning:
   13. Conduct scenario planning exercises to prepare for various potential challenges. This helps you anticipate and react to different situations effectively.

Remember that risk is inherent in business, and it's impossible to eliminate all risks completely. However, by following these strategies and maintaining a proactive approach, you can minimize the impact of risks and navigate challenges more effectively.

12.1 Common Startup Challenges

Starting a new business can be an exciting venture, but it's also accompanied by a range of common challenges. Being aware of these challenges and having strategies to address them can greatly improve your chances of success. Here are some common startup challenges:

1. **Market Research and Validation:**
   1. Many startups fail because they haven't thoroughly researched their target market or validated their business idea. It's crucial to understand your customers and their needs.

2. **Funding and Capital Constraints:**
   2. Access to capital is often a significant challenge for startups. You may need to secure funding through investors, loans, or personal savings to get your business off the ground.

3. **Competition:**
   3. In most industries, there is competition. You'll need a clear strategy to differentiate your product or service and stand out from competitors.

4. **Hiring and Building a Team:**
   4. Attracting and retaining the right talent can be challenging, especially if you're a small startup with limited resources. Building a strong team is essential for growth.

5. **Legal and Regulatory Compliance:**
   5. Navigating the legal and regulatory landscape can be complex and costly. Ensure that your business complies with all relevant laws and regulations.

6. **Cash Flow Management:**
   6. Managing cash flow is critical, as many startups struggle with inconsistent revenue and high expenses. Careful financial planning and budgeting are essential.
7. **Marketing and Customer Acquisition:**
   7. Getting the word out about your business and acquiring customers can be difficult and expensive. Develop a solid marketing strategy to reach your target audience.
8. **Product Development and Iteration:**
   8. Building a product or service that meets customer needs and continually improving it based on feedback is an ongoing challenge.
9. **Scaling and Growth:**
   9. Scaling a business while maintaining quality and profitability is a common challenge. You'll need to plan for growth and manage it effectively.
10. **Technology and Infrastructure:**
    10. Many startups rely on technology, and ensuring that your IT infrastructure is secure and scalable is vital. Cybersecurity is a growing concern.
11. **Risk Management:**
    11. Startups often face uncertainty and risk. Developing a risk management strategy is essential to mitigate potential setbacks.
12. **Sales and Revenue Generation:**
    12. Generating consistent sales and revenue is a constant challenge. You may need to experiment with different sales channels and strategies to find what works best.
13. **Time Management and Work-Life Balance:**
    13. Startup founders often work long hours, which can lead to burnout. Balancing work and personal life is essential for long-term success.
14. **Market Fluctuations:**
    14. Economic and market conditions can change rapidly. Being adaptable and prepared for market fluctuations is crucial.
15. **Mental Health and Stress:**
    15. The stress and uncertainty of running a startup can take a toll on mental health. It's important to recognize the signs of burnout and take steps to maintain your well-being.

To overcome these challenges, it's important to create a well-thought-out business plan, seek advice and mentorship, and continuously adapt your strategies as your business evolves. It's also valuable to build a strong support network and be prepared for the unexpected, as entrepreneurship often involves facing unforeseen obstacles.

12.2 Risk Management

Risk management is a systematic process of identifying, assessing, prioritizing, and mitigating risks to minimize their potential negative impact on an organization. It is an essential practice in both business and other fields to ensure the achievement of objectives, protect assets, and enhance decision-making. Here are the key components of risk management:

1. **Risk Identification:**
   1. The first step is to identify potential risks that could affect your organization. This includes internal and external risks, such as financial risks, operational risks, compliance risks, and strategic risks.
2. **Risk Assessment:**
   2. Once identified, risks are assessed to determine their potential impact and likelihood. This is often done through quantitative and qualitative analysis to prioritize risks.
3. **Risk Prioritization:**
   3. Not all risks are equally important. Organizations prioritize risks based on their potential impact and probability. High-priority risks require more immediate attention and resources.
4. **Risk Mitigation and Control:**
   4. After prioritizing risks, organizations develop strategies to mitigate or control them. This may involve risk avoidance (eliminating the risk), risk reduction (minimizing the impact or likelihood), risk transfer (e.g., insurance), or risk acceptance (if the risk is deemed acceptable).
5. **Monitoring and Review:**
   5. Risk management is an ongoing process. Regularly monitor and review the risk landscape to identify new risks and assess the effectiveness of existing risk mitigation measures.
6. **Risk Reporting and Communication:**
   6. Effective communication of risk information is critical. Stakeholders need to be informed about risks and the measures

being taken to manage them. Transparent reporting ensures that everyone is on the same page.

7. **Risk Culture and Governance:**
   7. Establish a risk-aware culture within the organization. Encourage employees to report risks and ensure that risk management is integrated into the governance structure.

8. **Compliance and Regulations:**
   8. Ensure that your risk management practices comply with relevant laws and regulations. This is particularly important in industries with strict regulatory oversight.

9. **Financial Risk Management:**
   9. Manage financial risks such as market risk, credit risk, liquidity risk, and currency risk to protect the organization's financial health.

10. **Operational Risk Management:**
    10. Address operational risks related to internal processes, technology, supply chain, and human resources. This includes contingency planning and disaster recovery.

11. **Strategic Risk Management:**
    11. Manage strategic risks that could impact the organization's long-term goals and competitive position. This involves scenario planning and adaptation.

12. **Cybersecurity Risk Management:**
    12. Protect against cybersecurity risks, which are increasingly important in our digital world. This includes measures to safeguard data and prevent cyberattacks.

13. **Environmental and Social Risk Management:**
    13. Address environmental and social risks, especially important for organizations with a focus on sustainability and corporate social responsibility.

14. **Third-Party Risk Management:**
    14. Evaluate and manage risks associated with third-party relationships, including suppliers, contractors, and outsourcing partners.

15. **Insurance:**
    15. Consider purchasing insurance policies to transfer certain risks to an insurer, such as liability insurance, property insurance, and business interruption insurance.

Effective risk management is a dynamic and continuous process. It's about making informed decisions to strike a balance between taking risks for potential rewards and safeguarding against potential harm. It should be integrated into the strategic planning and operations of an organization to help achieve its objectives while minimizing the negative impact of uncertainties.

12.3 Crisis Management

Crisis management is a strategic approach to dealing with significant, unexpected events that have the potential to disrupt an organization's operations, reputation, or stakeholder relationships. These crises can come in various forms, such as natural disasters, public relations disasters, cybersecurity breaches, financial crises, and more. Effective crisis management involves planning, response, and recovery phases. Here are the key components of crisis management:

1. **Preparation and Planning:**
   1. Develop a comprehensive crisis management plan before a crisis occurs. This plan should outline roles, responsibilities, communication protocols, and strategies for various types of crises.
2. **Risk Assessment:**
   2. Identify potential risks and vulnerabilities that could lead to a crisis. Assess the likelihood and potential impact of these risks to prioritize preparedness efforts.
3. **Crisis Team Formation:**
   3. Establish a crisis management team composed of key individuals from various departments. This team should include leaders, communication experts, and subject matter experts.
4. **Communication Plan:**
   4. Develop a crisis communication plan that outlines how the organization will communicate with internal and external stakeholders during a crisis. This includes drafting key messages and selecting communication channels.
5. **Training and Drills:**
   5. Regularly train your crisis management team and conduct drills or simulations to test the effectiveness of your crisis plan. This helps team members understand their roles and responsibilities and improves response time.
6. **Monitoring and Early Detection:**

6. Implement systems to monitor potential triggers or early warning signs of a crisis, such as social media monitoring, cybersecurity threat detection, and weather alerts.

7. **Immediate Response:**
   7. When a crisis occurs, initiate your crisis plan immediately. Focus on ensuring the safety of people, preserving assets, and stabilizing the situation.

8. **Communication and Transparency:**
   8. Communicate with stakeholders, including employees, customers, the media, and the public, as soon as possible. Transparency is key to maintaining trust during a crisis.

9. **Adaptive Leadership:**
   9. Crisis leaders should exhibit strong, adaptive leadership qualities, making quick decisions, remaining calm, and guiding the team through the crisis.

10. **Resource Allocation:**
    10. Allocate necessary resources to manage the crisis effectively. This includes financial resources, personnel, and technology.

11. **Legal and Regulatory Compliance:**
    11. Ensure that your response to the crisis complies with relevant laws and regulations. This is particularly important in highly regulated industries.

12. **Recovery Planning:**
    12. Develop a recovery plan to transition from the immediate response phase to the long-term recovery phase. This includes rebuilding, restoring operations, and reputation management.

13. **Review and Learning:**
    13. After the crisis, conduct a thorough review of what went well and what could be improved. Use the lessons learned to update and enhance your crisis management plan.

14. **Stakeholder Support:**
    14. Provide support to affected stakeholders, such as employees and customers, both during and after the crisis. This helps rebuild trust and loyalty.

15. **Media Relations:**
    15. Work closely with the media to ensure accurate and timely reporting. Develop relationships with reporters and be prepared for press conferences and interviews.

Crisis management is not just about reacting to an event but also about proactively preparing for the unexpected. An effective crisis management plan can help minimize the impact of a crisis on an organization and protect its reputation, brand, and long-term viability. It is a critical aspect of good corporate governance and responsible leadership.

12.4 Adapting to Market Changes

Adapting to market changes is a crucial aspect of staying competitive and sustainable in business. Markets are dynamic, and they can evolve rapidly due to factors such as technological advancements, changes in consumer behavior, economic shifts, and global events. Here are strategies for adapting to market changes effectively:

1. **Continuous Market Research:**
   - Stay informed about market trends, consumer preferences, and industry developments through ongoing market research. Regularly analyze data and feedback to identify emerging changes.
2. **Flexibility and Agility:**
   - Cultivate a flexible organizational culture that can quickly respond to market shifts. Be willing to adapt and change course as necessary.
3. **Customer-Centric Approach:**
   - Focus on understanding and meeting the changing needs and desires of your customers. Collect feedback and engage with them to provide tailored solutions.
4. **Product or Service Innovation:**
   - Innovate to create new products or services that address emerging market demands. This can involve improving existing offerings or diversifying your portfolio.
5. **Competitive Analysis:**
   - Monitor your competitors and be aware of their strategies. Analyze their successes and failures to inform your own decisions.
6. **Digital Transformation:**
   - Embrace technology and digital solutions to keep pace with market changes. Invest in e-commerce, digital marketing, and automation to enhance your efficiency and reach.

7. **Strategic Planning:**
   - Regularly revisit and update your business strategies to align with changing market conditions. This includes setting new goals and KPIs based on the evolving landscape.
8. **Risk Management:**
   - Develop a risk management strategy to mitigate potential challenges and uncertainties that market changes can bring. Be prepared for various scenarios.
9. **Customer Segmentation:**
   - Segment your customer base to tailor your marketing and sales efforts to different groups with distinct needs and preferences.
10. **Supply Chain Diversification:**
    - Diversify your supply chain and sourcing options to mitigate disruptions caused by changes in geopolitical or economic conditions.
11. **Adaptive Marketing:**
    - Adjust your marketing and advertising strategies to target new customer segments or address shifting consumer behaviors. Be prepared to experiment with different marketing channels.
12. **Data Analytics:**
    - Leverage data analytics to gain insights into customer behavior, market trends, and emerging opportunities. Data-driven decision-making is vital for adapting to changes.
13. **Talent Development:**
    - Invest in employee training and development to ensure your team has the skills and knowledge necessary to navigate market shifts.
14. **Collaboration and Partnerships:**
    - Collaborate with other businesses or industry partners to share resources and insights. Partnerships can help you adapt more effectively to market changes.
15. **Sustainability and Corporate Social Responsibility (CSR):**
    - Be attuned to growing environmental and social consciousness in the market. Incorporating sustainability and CSR initiatives can enhance your brand's reputation.
16. **Regulatory Compliance:**

- Stay informed about changes in regulations that may impact your industry. Ensure your business is in compliance to avoid legal and financial issues.

17. Scenario Planning:
- Develop scenarios that explore potential market changes and their impact on your business. These scenarios can guide your strategic decision-making.

Adapting to market changes requires a proactive and forward-thinking approach. It's not enough to react to changes after they occur; successful businesses anticipate and prepare for them. Embracing change as an opportunity for growth and improvement is a key mindset for adapting effectively in dynamic markets.

Measuring success can vary greatly depending on the context, whether it's in your personal life, career, business, or any other area. Success is subjective and can be defined in various ways, depending on individual goals and values. Here are some common methods and considerations for measuring success:

1. **Goal Achievement:** Many people measure success by accomplishing specific goals they've set for themselves. These goals can be short-term or long-term, and they may relate to personal, professional, or academic aspirations.
2. **Financial Success:** For some, financial prosperity is a primary measure of success. This includes factors like income, savings, investments, and overall financial stability.
3. **Career Advancement:** Career success may involve factors such as promotions, job satisfaction, job security, and achieving a particular position or status in your field.
4. **Personal Fulfillment:** Success can also be measured by how happy and fulfilled you feel in your personal life. This can encompass relationships, hobbies, health, and overall well-being.
5. **Impact and Contribution:** Many people view success as the positive impact they've had on others or on society as a whole. This might include volunteering, charitable work, or making a difference in your community.

6. **Learning and Growth:** Continuous learning and personal growth are often indicators of success. This could involve acquiring new skills, gaining knowledge, or evolving as a person over time.
7. **Quality of Life:** Success might be defined by your overall quality of life, encompassing factors like work-life balance, stress levels, and how well you're able to enjoy life outside of work.
8. **Happiness and Contentment:** Your own sense of happiness and contentment with your life is a subjective but important measure of success. How satisfied you are with your life can be a strong indicator.
9. **Legacy:** Some individuals measure success by considering the legacy they leave behind, such as the impact they've had on future generations or the lasting effects of their work.
10. **Peer and Self-Comparison:** Success can also be measured by comparing yourself to your peers or your past self. This can be motivating for some but may lead to negative feelings for others.
11. **Feedback and Recognition:** Positive feedback and recognition from others, whether it's in your personal life or at work, can be a form of measuring success.
12. **Balance and Well-Roundedness:** Striving for balance and being well-rounded can be another approach to success. This includes maintaining a harmonious life across various areas, such as career, family, personal interests, and health.

It's important to remember that success is highly individual and subjective. What constitutes success for one person may not be the same for another. It's also important to periodically reassess your goals and values, as they may evolve over time. Ultimately, success is about aligning your actions and achievements with your own vision of a fulfilling and meaningful life.

13.1 Key Performance Indicators (KPIs)

Key Performance Indicators (KPIs) are specific, measurable metrics used to evaluate the performance of an individual, team, department, or organization in achieving its goals and objectives. KPIs play a crucial role in providing quantifiable data to assess progress, identify areas for improvement, and make informed decisions. The selection of KPIs depends on the nature and goals of the organization or project. Here are some common categories of KPIs:

1. **Financial KPIs:**
   - **Revenue:** Measures the total income generated.
   - **Profit Margin:** Indicates the profitability by comparing revenue to expenses.
   - **Cost of Goods Sold (COGS):** Tracks the cost of producing goods or services.
   - **Return on Investment (ROI):** Evaluates the return on investment from various initiatives.
   - **Cash Flow:** Measures the inflow and outflow of cash within a specific period.
2. **Customer KPIs:**
   - **Customer Satisfaction (CSAT):** Measures the level of satisfaction among customers.
   - **Net Promoter Score (NPS):** Evaluates customer loyalty and likelihood to recommend.
   - **Customer Acquisition Cost (CAC):** Assesses the cost of acquiring a new customer.
   - **Customer Retention Rate:** Measures the rate at which customers continue doing business with the company.
   - **Average Revenue Per User (ARPU):** Calculates the average income generated per customer.
3. **Marketing and Sales KPIs:**
   - **Conversion Rate:** Evaluates the percentage of leads that convert into customers.
   - **Lead Generation:** Measures the number of new leads or prospects.
   - **Sales Growth:** Tracks the increase in sales over a specific period.
   - **Website Traffic:** Measures the number of visitors to a website.
   - **Cost Per Click (CPC) or Cost Per Acquisition (CPA):** Assesses the cost of acquiring website visitors or customers through advertising.
4. **Operational KPIs:**
   - **Inventory Turnover:** Evaluates how quickly inventory is sold and replenished.
   - **On-Time Delivery:** Measures the punctuality of delivering products or services.

- **Quality Metrics:** Tracks the quality and accuracy of products or services.
- **Downtime:** Measures the time during which machinery or systems are not operational.

5. **Employee KPIs:**
   - **Employee Turnover Rate:** Measures the percentage of employees who leave the organization.
   - **Employee Productivity:** Evaluates the output or performance of employees.
   - **Employee Satisfaction:** Assesses the job satisfaction and morale of employees.
   - **Training and Development:** Measures the progress and effectiveness of training programs.
6. **Project Management KPIs:**
   - **Project Timeline:** Tracks project progress against the planned schedule.
   - **Budget Variance:** Measures the variance between the budgeted and actual costs.
   - **Scope Changes:** Evaluates the number of changes to the project scope.
   - **Quality of Deliverables:** Assesses the quality and completeness of project deliverables.
7. **Healthcare KPIs:**
   - **Patient Satisfaction:** Measures the level of patient satisfaction with healthcare services.
   - **Readmission Rate:** Tracks the rate at which patients are readmitted after discharge.
   - **Average Length of Stay:** Evaluates the average number of days a patient spends in the hospital.
   - **Mortality Rate:** Measures the rate of patient deaths within a specific time frame.

KPIs should be specific, measurable, achievable, relevant, and time-bound (SMART) to be effective. They should also align with an organization's strategic objectives and provide actionable insights for decision-making. Regularly monitoring and adjusting KPIs is essential to drive continuous improvement and achieve success in various aspects of business and operations.

Analyzing financial metrics is essential for assessing the financial health and performance of a company or organization. By examining various financial metrics, you can gain insights into the company's profitability, liquidity, solvency, and overall financial stability. Here are some key financial metrics to analyze and the insights they can provide:

1. **Revenue:**
   - **Insight:** Revenue is the total income generated from sales of products or services.
   - **Analysis:** Analyzing revenue trends can indicate the company's sales growth or decline. It's essential to compare revenue to previous periods or industry benchmarks.
2. **Gross Profit Margin:**
   - **Insight:** Gross profit margin measures the profitability of a company's core operations.
   - **Analysis:** A declining margin may signal cost overruns or pricing pressure, while an increasing margin indicates efficient operations.
3. **Operating Profit Margin:**
   - **Insight:** Operating profit margin assesses the profitability of a company's core business operations, excluding non-operating expenses.
   - **Analysis:** A healthy operating margin is essential for long-term sustainability and growth.
4. **Net Profit Margin:**
   - **Insight:** Net profit margin reflects the profitability of the company after all expenses, including taxes.
   - **Analysis:** A positive net profit margin indicates profitability, while a negative margin suggests losses.
5. **Earnings Before Interest and Taxes (EBIT):**
   - **Insight:** EBIT measures a company's earnings before interest and taxes.
   - **Analysis:** EBIT helps assess the company's operational profitability, independent of financing and tax-related factors.
6. **Earnings Before Interest, Taxes, Depreciation, and Amortization (EBITDA):**

- **Insight:** EBITDA provides a more comprehensive view of a company's operating performance, excluding depreciation and amortization.
- **Analysis:** EBITDA is often used to assess the cash-generating ability of a company's core operations.

7. **Return on Assets (ROA):**
   - **Insight:** ROA measures the company's ability to generate profit from its total assets.
   - **Analysis:** A higher ROA suggests more efficient asset utilization.

8. **Return on Equity (ROE):**
   - **Insight:** ROE evaluates the company's ability to generate profit for its shareholders' equity.
   - **Analysis:** A high ROE typically indicates effective use of equity capital.

9. **Current Ratio:**
   - **Insight:** The current ratio assesses the company's ability to meet short-term liabilities with short-term assets.
   - **Analysis:** A ratio above 1 indicates good short-term liquidity, while below 1 may suggest liquidity issues.

10. **Debt-to-Equity Ratio:**
    - **Insight:** The debt-to-equity ratio measures the proportion of debt to equity in the company's capital structure.
    - **Analysis:** A high ratio may indicate a heavy debt burden, which could pose financial risk.

11. **Quick Ratio (Acid-Test Ratio):**
    - **Insight:** The quick ratio measures a company's ability to cover short-term liabilities with its most liquid assets (excluding inventory).
    - **Analysis:** A ratio above 1 suggests better short-term liquidity.

12. **Inventory Turnover:**
    - **Insight:** Inventory turnover evaluates how quickly a company sells its inventory.
    - **Analysis:** A higher turnover ratio implies efficient inventory management.

13. **Accounts Receivable Days:**
    - **Insight:** Accounts receivable days measure the average number of days it takes to collect on accounts receivable.

- **Analysis:** A shorter collection period indicates effective credit management.
14. **Cash Flow Metrics (Operating, Investing, and Financing):**
    - **Insight:** Cash flow metrics evaluate the sources and uses of cash within the company.
    - **Analysis:** Positive operating cash flow and adequate investing and financing cash flows are essential for financial sustainability.
15. **Market Metrics (Price-to-Earnings, Price-to-Sales, Price-to-Book, etc.):**
    - **Insight:** Market metrics relate the company's financial performance to its market value.
    - **Analysis:** These metrics can help assess whether a company is overvalued or undervalued in the stock market.

When analyzing financial metrics, it's important to consider historical trends, industry benchmarks, and the company's specific circumstances. Financial ratios and metrics should be viewed in context and compared to relevant industry standards to draw meaningful conclusions about a company's financial performance and stability.

13.3 Customer Feedback and Satisfaction

Customer feedback and satisfaction are crucial components of any successful business. Understanding what your customers think and feel about your products, services, and overall experience is essential for improving and growing your business. Here's how to effectively gather and utilize customer feedback and measure satisfaction:

1. **Gathering Customer Feedback:**
   a. **Surveys:** Create online or in-person surveys that include questions about specific aspects of your products or services. Use tools like SurveyMonkey or Google Forms to collect and analyze responses.
   b. **Feedback Forms:** Provide feedback forms on your website or in your physical locations. These can be as simple as a comment box or a rating system.
   c. **Social Media:** Monitor social media platforms for mentions, comments, and direct messages from customers. Respond to both positive and negative feedback.

d. **Customer Reviews:** Encourage customers to leave reviews on platforms like Yelp, Google Reviews, or industry-specific review sites. Pay attention to the feedback and respond appropriately.

e. **Email and Online Reviews:** Send post-purchase or post-service emails asking for feedback. Include a link to a feedback form or a review platform.

f. **Focus Groups:** Conduct focus groups to gather in-depth insights from a small group of customers. This can provide more qualitative data.

g. **Customer Service Interactions:** Train your customer service team to proactively ask for feedback during customer interactions, and document this feedback for analysis.

h. **In-App or In-Product Feedback:** If you have digital products or apps, use in-app prompts to collect feedback on specific features or user experiences.

2. **Analyzing Customer Feedback:**

a. **Categorize Feedback:** Group feedback into categories such as product quality, customer service, website usability, etc. This helps identify common themes.

b. **Sentiment Analysis:** Use natural language processing tools to determine the sentiment of the feedback—positive, negative, or neutral.

c. **Identify Trends:** Look for recurring issues or praise. This can help you prioritize areas for improvement.

d. **Quantitative Metrics:** Analyze numerical ratings or scores to track changes in customer satisfaction over time.

3. **Measuring Customer Satisfaction:**

a. **Net Promoter Score (NPS):** Ask customers how likely they are to recommend your business to others on a scale of 0-10. Calculate the NPS by subtracting the percentage of detractors (0-6) from promoters (9-10).

b. **Customer Satisfaction Score (CSAT):** Use a simple rating scale to ask customers how satisfied they are with your product or service.

c. **Customer Effort Score (CES):** Measure how easy it is for customers to achieve their goals when interacting with your company.

d. **Repeat Business:** High levels of repeat business and customer retention are indicative of customer satisfaction.

4. **Taking Action Based on Feedback:**
   a. **Address Issues:** Act on the feedback by addressing specific issues or concerns raised by customers. Provide solutions and follow up.
   b. **Continuous Improvement:** Use feedback to make ongoing improvements to your products, services, and customer experience.
   c. **Recognition and Rewards:** Acknowledge and reward employees who receive positive feedback or who go above and beyond to satisfy customers.
   d. **Communication:** Keep customers informed about changes or improvements made as a result of their feedback.
   e. **Closed-Loop Feedback:** Implement a system where you follow up with customers after resolving issues to ensure they are satisfied with the resolution.
5. **Monitoring Trends:**
   a. Continuously track and monitor customer feedback and satisfaction to identify long-term trends and areas that may require ongoing attention.
6. **Benchmarking:**
   a. Compare your customer satisfaction metrics with industry benchmarks to see how you stack up against competitors.
7. **Employee Training and Engagement:**
   a. Invest in training and engaging employees in customer service to ensure they can address customer concerns effectively and maintain high satisfaction levels.

Customer feedback and satisfaction are valuable resources for improving your business and building strong customer relationships. By actively seeking feedback, analyzing it, and taking action, you can enhance your products and services while fostering customer loyalty and trust.

13.4 Adjusting Your Strategy

Adjusting your strategy is a crucial aspect of effective decision-making, whether you're managing a business, project, or personal goals. Adapting your strategy allows you to respond to changing circumstances, improve performance, and achieve your objectives. Here's a step-by-step guide on how to adjust your strategy:

1. **Assess the Current Situation:**
   - Begin by evaluating your current situation. What factors have changed since you initially formulated your strategy? This may include shifts in the market, customer preferences, competition, or internal challenges.
2. **Review Your Goals and Objectives:**
   - Revisit your long-term and short-term goals. Are they still relevant and achievable given the new circumstances? Ensure your goals align with your organization's mission and values.
3. **Analyze Data and Feedback:**
   - Gather and analyze relevant data, such as financial reports, customer feedback, market research, and performance metrics. This information provides valuable insights into what is working and what needs adjustment.
4. **Identify Strengths and Weaknesses:**
   - Conduct a SWOT analysis (Strengths, Weaknesses, Opportunities, Threats) to identify internal and external factors affecting your strategy. This helps you recognize areas where you excel and areas needing improvement.
5. **Assess Risk and Uncertainty:**
   - Consider the potential risks and uncertainties associated with your strategy. Identify contingencies and risk mitigation plans to address these challenges.
6. **Engage Stakeholders:**
   - Involve key stakeholders, such as employees, customers, partners, and advisors, in the strategy adjustment process. Their perspectives and insights can provide a well-rounded view of the situation.
7. **Generate Alternative Strategies:**
   - Brainstorm different strategies that could address the new challenges or opportunities. Don't limit yourself to one approach; consider several alternatives.
8. **Evaluate Alternative Strategies:**
   - Assess the pros and cons of each alternative strategy. Consider their feasibility, potential impact, and alignment with your goals and values.
9. **Select the Best Strategy:**

- Based on your evaluation, choose the strategy that appears to be the most promising and suitable for your situation. It should address the identified issues and align with your objectives.

10. **Develop an Action Plan:**
    - Create a detailed action plan outlining the steps needed to implement your chosen strategy. Set clear objectives, deadlines, and responsibilities.

11. **Allocate Resources:**
    - Ensure you have the necessary resources, including financial, human, and technological, to execute the strategy effectively.

12. **Communication and Change Management:**
    - Communicate the changes to all relevant stakeholders. Ensure they understand the rationale behind the new strategy and how it impacts them. Implement change management strategies to ease the transition.

13. **Monitor Progress and KPIs:**
    - Establish key performance indicators (KPIs) and metrics to track the progress of your adjusted strategy. Regularly review these indicators to measure success and identify areas that require further adjustment.

14. **Continuous Evaluation and Adaptation:**
    - Strategy adjustment is an ongoing process. Continuously monitor the external environment, your internal operations, and the performance of your strategy. Be prepared to adapt as needed.

15. **Learn from Mistakes:**
    - Be open to learning from your mistakes and failures. Use them as opportunities to refine your strategy and make more informed decisions in the future.

Adjusting your strategy is a dynamic and iterative process. It's essential to stay flexible, responsive, and willing to change when circumstances demand it. By following these steps, you can ensure that your strategy remains aligned with your goals and adaptable to the evolving business landscape.

E xiting your business is a significant decision that requires careful planning and execution. There are several ways to exit a business, and the best method for you depends on your goals, the nature of your business, and your personal circumstances. Here are some common methods for exiting a business:

1. **Selling the Business:**
    - **Selling to a Strategic Buyer:** This involves selling your business to a larger company in the same industry, which can often result in a higher purchase price due to synergies.
    - **Selling to a Financial Buyer:** Financial buyers, such as private equity firms, may be interested in acquiring a profitable business. They often provide the owner with a partial stake or full exit.
2. **Passing it to Family or Successors:**
    1. If you have family members or employees who are interested in taking over the business, you can plan for a smooth transition through a sale or a gift.
3. **IPO (Initial Public Offering):**
    2. Taking the company public through an IPO is an option for larger, well-established businesses with significant growth potential.
4. **Liquidation:**

3. In this method, you sell off all the assets of the business, pay off the debts, and distribute any remaining proceeds to the owner(s). This is typically used when there is no buyer or successor.

5. **Mergers and Acquisitions (M&A):**
   4. Merging with or being acquired by another company can be a strategic exit for businesses looking to expand or combine resources.
6. **Management Buyout (MBO) or Employee Stock Ownership Plan (ESOP):**
   5. In an MBO, the management team buys the business from the owner. ESOPs are retirement plans that allow employees to acquire ownership in the business over time.
7. **Franchising:**
   6. If your business has a successful and replicable model, you can franchise it, allowing others to open and operate similar businesses under your brand.
8. **Closure or Bankruptcy:**
   7. Sometimes, businesses face insurmountable challenges and have to close down or declare bankruptcy. This is often the least desirable exit option.
9. **Strategic Partnerships or Joint Ventures:**
   8. Collaborating with another business through a partnership or joint venture can be a way to exit while maintaining some involvement or benefitting from the partnership.

When planning your exit strategy, it's important to consider factors such as your financial goals, the value of your business, market conditions, and the impact on employees, customers, and other stakeholders. Exit planning should begin well in advance of your desired exit date to maximize value and minimize potential complications. Consulting with financial advisors, legal professionals, and business brokers can help you navigate the complexities of exiting your business.

14.1 Selling Your Business

Selling your business can be a complex and multi-step process that requires careful planning and execution. Here are the key steps involved in selling your business:

1. **Determine Your Sale Objectives:**
   9. Before you start the process, clarify your objectives. Do you want to maximize profit, ensure the business continues to operate, or ensure your employees are taken care of? Your goals will influence the sales process.
2. **Business Valuation:**
   10. Determine the value of your business. This often involves financial analysis, considering assets, liabilities, revenue, profit, market conditions, and industry benchmarks. You may want to hire a professional appraiser or business broker for an accurate valuation.
3. **Clean Up Your Financials:**
   11. Ensure your financial records are in order. This includes tax returns, financial statements, and any outstanding legal or financial issues.
4. **Prepare a Business Profile:**
   12. Create a comprehensive business profile or prospectus that highlights the key aspects of your business. This should include financial data, company history, operations, customer base, and growth potential.
5. **Find a Qualified Business Broker or M&A Advisor:**
   13. Consider hiring a business broker or merger and acquisition (M&A) advisor. They can help you find potential buyers, negotiate the deal, and ensure confidentiality.
6. **Market Your Business:**
   14. Market your business discreetly to potential buyers. This may involve advertising, networking, or using a broker's network to find interested parties.
7. **Screen and Qualify Buyers:**
   15. Not all potential buyers will be a good fit for your business. Screen and qualify buyers to ensure they are serious and financially capable.
8. **Negotiate the Deal:**
   16. Negotiate the terms of the sale, including the purchase price, payment structure, and any contingencies. Be prepared for back-and-forth negotiations.
9. **Due Diligence:**

17. The buyer will conduct due diligence to review your business's records, contracts, assets, and liabilities. Be prepared to provide all necessary information and answer questions.

10. **Purchase Agreement:**
    18. Work with your attorney to draft a detailed purchase agreement that outlines the terms and conditions of the sale, including warranties and representations.

11. **Financing and Funding:**
    19. Determine how the buyer will finance the purchase. This may involve a combination of cash, loans, or seller financing.

12. **Obtain Necessary Approvals:**
    20. Depending on your business type and location, you may need to obtain regulatory approvals or permits for the sale.

13. **Closing the Deal:**
    21. Sign the final agreement, transfer ownership, and exchange funds. This may involve the transfer of physical assets, intellectual property, and other elements of the business.

14. **Transition and Handover:**
    22. Work out a transition plan with the buyer to ensure a smooth handover. This can include training, introducing the buyer to customers and suppliers, and ensuring a successful transfer of operations.

15. **Post-Sale Considerations:**
    23. After the sale, address any tax implications and decide what you will do with the proceeds. This might involve reinvesting, retirement planning, or other financial decisions.

Remember that selling a business can be a time-consuming and emotional process. It's essential to seek professional guidance from attorneys, accountants, and advisors who have experience in business sales. The process can take several months or even years, so patience and careful planning are key to a successful sale.

14.2 Passing It On

Passing on your business, whether to family members or key employees, is a significant decision that requires careful planning and execution. Here are the steps involved in passing on your business:

1. **Determine Your Succession Plan:**

1. Decide who you want to pass the business to. This could be family members, key employees, or a combination of both.
2. **Identify and Prepare Successors:**
    2. If you are passing the business to family members, ensure they have the necessary skills and experience to run the business. Provide them with training and mentorship if needed.
3. **Establish a Timeline:**
    3. Decide when you want to step down from the business. This might be a gradual process or a specific date.
4. **Create a Succession Plan:**
    4. Develop a detailed succession plan that outlines how the transition will occur. This should include leadership roles, responsibilities, and a timeline.
5. **Value the Business:**
    5. Determine the fair market value of your business. This is essential for estate planning and any financial arrangements with successors.
6. **Financial and Legal Considerations:**
    6. Work with financial advisors and legal professionals to structure the transfer in a tax-efficient manner. This might involve gifting, selling, or a combination of both.
7. **Business Structure:**
    7. Decide whether the transfer will be a gift, sale, or a combination of both. This decision can have significant tax implications.
8. **Communicate the Plan:**
    8. It's crucial to communicate the succession plan to all relevant parties, including family members and employees. Transparency can help reduce uncertainty and potential conflicts.
9. **Develop a Buy-Sell Agreement:**
    9. If you're passing the business to multiple family members or partners, a buy-sell agreement can be used to outline how ownership will be transferred in case of death, disability, or other triggering events.
10. **Funding the Transfer:**
    10. Determine how the successors will finance the purchase, whether through personal savings, loans, or seller financing.
11. **Training and Transition:**
    11. Provide training and mentorship to the successors, gradually transitioning leadership responsibilities to them.

12. **Legal Documentation:**
    12. Work with an attorney to create the necessary legal documents, such as share transfer agreements or partnership agreements, to formalize the transfer.
13. **Estate Planning:**
    13. Ensure that your estate plan aligns with your succession plan. This may involve updating wills and trusts to reflect the transfer of business assets.
14. **Review and Adjust:**
    14. Periodically review and adjust the succession plan as needed, especially if circumstances change or the business evolves.
15. **Post-Transition Support:**
    15. Offer ongoing support and guidance to the successors to ensure the continued success of the business.

Passing on a business can be an emotional and complex process. It's important to involve experienced professionals, including financial advisors, accountants, and lawyers, to ensure the process is executed smoothly and in a way that benefits both the outgoing owner and the new leadership.

14.3 Closing a Business

Closing a business is a difficult decision but sometimes a necessary one. Here are the steps to follow when closing a business:

1. **Review Your Legal Obligations:**
   - Check your state and local regulations for the legal requirements related to closing a business. This can include notifying the government, settling taxes, and fulfilling any contractual obligations.
2. **Inform Stakeholders:**
   - Notify employees, customers, suppliers, and other stakeholders about your decision to close the business. This can help you manage relationships and fulfill contractual obligations.
3. **Set a Closing Date:**
   - Decide on a closing date. This should give you enough time to wind down operations, complete necessary tasks, and meet any legal obligations.
4. **Financial Assessment:**

- Take a detailed look at your financial situation. This includes settling outstanding debts, collecting money owed to the business, and ensuring that your books are up to date.

5. **Notify Government Agencies:**
    - Depending on your location and business structure, you may need to inform government agencies of your business closure. This includes filing final tax returns and canceling business licenses.

6. **Address Employee Matters:**

    - Inform your employees about the closure and discuss severance packages, final paychecks, and any other benefits they may be entitled to. Ensure that you adhere to employment laws in your area.

7. **Notify Suppliers and Creditors:**
    - Inform your suppliers and creditors about the closure. Work out payment arrangements and fulfill outstanding obligations.

8. **Sell or Liquidate Assets:**
    - Determine whether it's more advantageous to sell your business assets or liquidate them. This decision should be based on your financial situation and the potential value of your assets.

9. **Settle Contracts and Agreements:**
    - Review and settle any contracts or agreements that are still in effect, including leases, service contracts, and warranties. You may need to negotiate termination terms.

10. **Distribute Assets:**
    - Distribute remaining assets to shareholders, partners, or owners, in accordance with the business structure and applicable agreements.

11. **Cancel Licenses and Permits:**
    - Cancel any business licenses, permits, and registrations. This will help prevent future legal and financial obligations.

12. **Handle Taxes:**
    - Ensure that all tax obligations are met, including federal, state, and local taxes. You may need to file final tax returns and obtain tax clearance certificates if required in your jurisdiction.

13. **Notify Customers and Suppliers:**

- Let your customers and suppliers know that you're closing the business. Provide them with information on how to fulfill any remaining orders or contracts.

14. Close Business Bank Accounts:
- Close all business bank accounts and ensure that all outstanding checks and payments have cleared.

15. Store Business Records:
- Keep business records and documents for the legally required period, which may vary depending on your location. This is important for potential audits or legal issues.

16. Notify Your Insurer:
- Contact your business insurance provider to cancel or adjust your coverage.

17. Winding Down Operations:
- Gradually wind down operations, sell or dispose of assets, and settle outstanding obligations.

18. Inform the Community:
- Depending on your business's significance in the community, you may want to inform the local community about your closure.

19. Document Everything:

Keep detailed records of all actions taken during the closure process. This documentation can be important in case of legal or financial issues that may arise later.

Closing a business can be a complex process, and it's advisable to seek legal and financial advice to ensure that you follow all the necessary steps and meet your obligations. Additionally, consider consulting with a business attorney or a CPA with experience in business closures to help navigate the process.

Conclusion

The conclusion of a business startup book is typically a summarization of the key points, insights, and takeaways provided throughout the book. It serves as a final word of advice and encouragement for aspiring entrepreneurs and those looking to start their own businesses. Here's what you might expect to find in the conclusion of a business startup book:

1. **Recap of Key Concepts:** The conclusion should briefly recap the most important concepts and lessons covered in the book. This serves as a refresher for readers, reinforcing the main ideas presented in earlier chapters.
2. **Inspiration and Encouragement:** The author may use the conclusion to inspire and encourage readers to take action. This often includes success stories of entrepreneurs who overcame challenges and achieved their goals.
3. **Call to Action:** The conclusion might include a call to action, urging readers to apply what they've learned and take the first steps toward starting their own business. This could involve setting goals, creating a business plan, or seeking out resources and support.
4. **Acknowledgment of Challenges:** It's important to acknowledge that starting a business can be challenging, and the conclusion may address this reality. However, it should also emphasize that challenges can be overcome with determination and the right strategies.
5. **Emphasis on Lifelong Learning:** Many business startup books stress the importance of continuous learning and personal growth. The conclusion may highlight the value of ongoing education and skill development in the entrepreneurial journey.
6. Realistic Expectations: A good conclusion may also set realistic expectations for readers. Starting a business is not a guaranteed path to success, and the conclusion should make it clear that it requires hard work, adaptability, and perseverance.
7. **Gratitude and Acknowledgment:** Authors often express their gratitude to readers for choosing to read their book and may acknowledge the support of friends, family, and mentors in their own entrepreneurial journey.

8. **Looking Ahead:** The conclusion may touch on the future of the business and the opportunities that lie ahead. It might discuss scaling, innovation, or other possibilities for growth.
9. **Additional Resources:** Some conclusions provide a list of additional resources, books, websites, or organizations that readers can turn to for further guidance and support in their entrepreneurial endeavors.

In essence, the conclusion of a business startup book is a motivational and informative closing statement that leaves readers inspired and equipped with the knowledge and confidence to pursue their entrepreneurial dreams. It should tie together the book's themes and leave the reader with a sense of purpose and determination.

Celebrating Your Success

Celebrating your success is a crucial part of any endeavor, including business, personal goals, or achievements. It not only allows you to acknowledge your hard work and accomplishments but also provides motivation and a sense of fulfillment. Here are some key points on celebrating your success:

1. **Reflection:** Take time to reflect on your journey. Understand the milestones you've achieved and how far you've come. This reflection can help you appreciate your success even more.
2. **Reward Yourself:** Celebrate with a reward that is meaningful to you. It could be a treat, a special purchase, a vacation, or simply a day off to relax and recharge.
3. **Share Your Success:** Sharing your success with friends, family, or colleagues can be a wonderful way to celebrate. They can offer their congratulations and join in your joy.
4. **Gratitude:** Express gratitude to those who supported you along the way. Recognizing the contributions of others can enhance your celebration and strengthen your relationships.
5. **Set New Goals:** While celebrating, it's also a good time to think about what's next. Setting new goals can maintain your motivation and keep you moving forward.
6. **Document Your Success:** Create a journal or a visual reminder of your success. This can serve as a source of inspiration when you face challenges in the future.

7. **Learn from the Experience:** Reflect on what you've learned from the journey and how you can apply those lessons to future endeavors.
8. **Plan for the Future:** Use your success as a stepping stone to plan for a more successful future. This could involve scaling your business, personal growth, or helping others achieve their goals.
9. **Celebrate Small Wins:** Don't wait for major achievements to celebrate. Recognize and celebrate small wins along the way. This can provide ongoing motivation and make the journey more enjoyable.
10. **Maintain Balance:** While celebrating success is important, it's also crucial to maintain a healthy work-life balance. Don't get so caught up in celebrating that you neglect other aspects of your life.
11. **Self-Care:** Use the celebration as an opportunity for self-care. Take care of your physical and mental well-being to ensure you're ready for new challenges.
12. **Stay Humble:** While celebrating, it's important to remain humble and avoid arrogance. Success is a journey, and there will be ups and downs.

Remember that celebrating your success is not just about the destination but also about recognizing and appreciating the effort and dedication you put into achieving your goals. It's a way to stay motivated, maintain a positive outlook, and keep pushing forward toward new horizons.

The Continuous Entrepreneurial Journey

The entrepreneurial journey is not a one-time event but a continuous and dynamic process. It involves a series of steps, challenges, and opportunities that an entrepreneur faces throughout their career. Here are some key points that illustrate the continuous nature of the entrepreneurial journey:

1. **Starting and Scaling:** The journey typically begins with the idea and creation of a business. However, it doesn't end there. Entrepreneurs often aim to scale their businesses, expand into new markets, or introduce new products or services.
2. **Learning and Adaptation:** Entrepreneurship involves a steep learning curve. Entrepreneurs must continually acquire new skills,

adapt to changing market conditions, and stay updated on industry trends.

3. **Mistakes and Failures:** Failures and mistakes are inevitable in entrepreneurship. These setbacks can serve as valuable learning experiences, allowing entrepreneurs to make better decisions in the future.

4. **Innovation and Creativity:** Stagnation can be detrimental to a business. Successful entrepreneurs continually innovate and find creative solutions to problems, whether it's in product development, marketing, or operations.

5. **Market Changes:** Markets are dynamic and can change rapidly. Entrepreneurs need to stay attuned to shifts in consumer preferences, emerging technologies, and competitive landscapes.

6. **Networking and Relationships:** Building and maintaining relationships with customers, partners, investors, and mentors is an ongoing process. Networking and nurturing these connections can lead to valuable opportunities and support.

7. **Financial Management:** Financial stability is crucial for business sustainability. Entrepreneurs must continuously manage finances, monitor cash flow, and seek funding or investment when necessary.

8. **Goal Setting and Vision:** Entrepreneurial journeys are guided by goals and a long-term vision. Entrepreneurs should regularly revisit and update these objectives to ensure alignment with their business's current status and future ambitions.

9. **Work-Life Balance:** Balancing the demands of entrepreneurship with personal life is an ongoing challenge. Maintaining a healthy work-life balance is essential to avoid burnout and maintain well-being.

10. **Resilience and Determination:** Entrepreneurship can be a rollercoaster of ups and downs. Resilience and determination are essential to weather the challenges and setbacks that are an inherent part of the journey.

11. **Regulatory and Legal Compliance:** Staying compliant with evolving regulations and legal requirements is a constant responsibility, as non-compliance can have severe consequences for a business.

12. **Mentorship and Education:** Entrepreneurs often seek mentorship and education to improve their skills and decision-making. This pursuit of knowledge is a continuous process.

13. **Succession Planning:** At some point, entrepreneurs may consider succession planning, whether it's passing the business to the next generation or selling it. This planning is another aspect of the long-term entrepreneurial journey.
14. **Legacy and Impact:** Some entrepreneurs aim to leave a lasting legacy or make a positive impact on society. This aspect of the journey extends well beyond the immediate business success.

In essence, the entrepreneurial journey is a marathon, not a sprint. It's marked by its continuity, challenges, and the need for adaptability. Successful entrepreneurs embrace the idea that the journey never truly ends but rather evolves and unfolds in new and exciting ways as they continue to pursue their goals and aspirations.

Appendix

Entrepreneurship can be a rewarding but challenging journey, and there are many resources available to help aspiring and established entrepreneurs. Here are some key resources to consider:

1. **Online Courses and Tutorials:**
   - **Coursera:** Offers a wide range of courses on entrepreneurship, business strategy, and related topics.
   - **edX:** Provides courses from top universities and institutions on entrepreneurship and business management.
   - **Udemy:** Offers a variety of affordable courses on entrepreneurship and related skills.
2. **Books:**
   - "The Lean Startup" by Eric Ries: A classic for anyone looking to build a startup.
   - "Zero to One" by Peter Thiel: Offers insights on startups and innovation.
   - "Good to Great" by Jim Collins: Focuses on turning good companies into great ones.
3. **Online Communities:**
   - **Reddit's /r/Entrepreneur:** A large community of entrepreneurs sharing advice and experiences.
   - **Indie Hackers:** Focused on solo founders and small startups.
   - **LinkedIn Groups:** There are many entrepreneurship-related groups where you can network and seek advice.
4. **Startup Incubators and Accelerators:**
   - Look for local or global programs that offer funding, mentorship, and resources to startups.
   - Y Combinator, 500 Startups, and Techstars are some prominent global accelerators.
5. **Government and Nonprofit Organizations:**
   - Many governments and nonprofit organizations offer grants, loans, and support for startups.
   - Check with your local chamber of commerce or Small Business Administration (SBA).
6. **Networking Events and Conferences:**
   - Attend industry-specific conferences, meetups, and networking events to connect with other entrepreneurs.

- Events like TechCrunch Disrupt and Web Summit are popular in the tech startup space.
7. **Online Tools and Platforms:**
   - **HubSpot:** Offers a suite of tools for marketing, sales, and customer relationship management.
   - **Shopify:** A popular platform for e-commerce businesses.
   - **Stripe:** Provides payment processing solutions for online businesses.
8. **Mentorship Programs:**
   - Look for experienced entrepreneurs who are willing to mentor you.
   - Organizations like SCORE provide free business mentoring.
9. **Financial Resources:**
   - Explore crowdfunding platforms like Kickstarter and Indiegogo.
   - Angel investors and venture capitalists can provide funding for your startup.
10. **Blogs and Podcasts:**
    - Blogs like "StartUp" by Gimlet Media and podcasts like "How I Built This" by NPR share inspiring startup stories.
    - Reading blogs like "Entrepreneur" or "Inc." Can also provide valuable insights.
11. **Online Tools for Project Management and Collaboration:**
    - Tools like Trello, Asana, and Slack can help you manage your projects and collaborate with your team effectively.
12. **Legal and Regulatory Guidance:**
    - Consult with a business attorney to ensure you're meeting all legal requirements and protecting your intellectual property.
13. **Market Research Tools:**
    - Tools like Google Trends, SEMrush, and SurveyMonkey can help you understand your target market and competition.
14. **Co-Working Spaces:**
    - If you need an office space, co-working spaces like WeWork and local alternatives can provide an affordable and flexible option.
15. **Funding Platforms:**
    - Consider crowdfunding platforms like Kickstarter and Indiegogo for early-stage funding.
16. **Business Plan Templates:**

- Many online resources provide free business plan templates to help you structure your ideas and seek funding.

17. **Social Media and Online Marketing Resources:**
    - Hootsuite, Buffer, and Google Ads can help with social media management and online advertising.

18. **Financial and Accounting Software:**
    - QuickBooks, Xero, and FreshBooks are popular choices for managing finances and accounting.

19. **Educational and Networking Events:**
    - Attend local meetups, industry conferences, and workshops to expand your knowledge and network.

20. **Startup News Outlets:**
    - Keep up with the latest trends and news through platforms like TechCrunch, Mashable, and Entrepreneur.

Remember that the specific resources you need will depend on your industry, location, and the stage of your entrepreneurial journey. It's also essential to continuously adapt and learn from your experiences to succeed as an entrepreneur.

Business Plan Template

Creating a business plan is a crucial step for any entrepreneur, whether you're starting a new business or seeking to grow an existing one. A well-structured business plan can help you outline your business concept, set goals, secure funding, and guide your company's growth. Below, you'll find a basic business plan template to get you started. Feel free to adapt it to your specific needs and industry:

1. **Executive Summary:**
    - Provide a concise overview of your business, including your mission, vision, and core values.
    - Summarize the key points of your business plan.

2. **Business Description:**
    - Explain your business idea and its purpose.
    - Describe your products or services.
    - Mention the problem your business solves or the need it fulfills.

3. **Market Research:**
    - Present market analysis, including industry trends, target market demographics, and competition.
    - Describe your target customer and their needs.

4. **Marketing and Sales Strategy:**
    - Outline your marketing approach, including branding, advertising, and customer acquisition.
    - Explain your sales strategy, pricing, and distribution channels.
5. **Organization and Management:**
    - Detail your company's structure, ownership, and key team members.
    - Include resumes of key personnel with relevant experience.
6. **Product or Service Line:**
    - Provide in-depth information about your products or services.
    - Highlight their unique selling points.
7. **Funding Request (if applicable):**
    - Specify the amount of funding you need and how you'll use it.
    - Include your financial projections and expected ROI for potential investors.
8. **Financial Projections:**
    - Present financial statements, including income statements, cash flow statements, and balance sheets.
    - Provide sales forecasts, break-even analysis, and a budget.
9. **Appendix:**
    - Include any additional information that supports your business plan, such as market research data, legal documents, and charts/graphs.
10. **SWOT Analysis:**
    - Analyze your business's strengths, weaknesses, opportunities, and threats.
11. **Milestones and Timelines:**
    - Outline your business milestones and set realistic timelines for achieving them.

Remember that your business plan should be tailored to your specific needs and goals. Depending on your audience, such as potential investors or lenders, you may need to focus more on financial projections and the funding request section.

Additionally, it's important to keep your business plan concise and engaging. While the template above provides a general structure, feel free to customize it to make your business plan stand out and effectively communicate your vision and strategy.

Sure, here's an example of simplified financial statements in text format for a fictional business. These financial statements include an Income Statement, Balance Sheet, and Cash Flow Statement.

Income Statement (Profit and Loss Statement) for the Year Ended December 31, 20XX:

1. Yaml
   - **Revenue:** $500,000
   - **Cost of Goods Sold:** $250,000
   - **Gross Profit:** $250,000

Operating Expenses:

- Salaries and Wages: $100,000
- Rent: $20,000
- Utilities: $5,000
- Marketing and Advertising: $30,000
- Depreciation: $10,000
- Other Operating Expenses: $15,000

Total Operating Expenses: $180,000

- Operating Income: $70,000
- Other Income and Expenses:
- Interest Income: $5,000
- Interest Expense: $8,000
- Miscellaneous Income: $2,000
- Miscellaneous Expenses: $1,000
- Net Other Income/Expenses: -$2,000
- Net Income Before Tax: $68,000
- Income Tax Expense: $20,000
- Net Income: $48,00

Balance Sheet as of December 31, 20XX:

2. Yaml

Assets:

- Cash and Cash Equivalents: $30,000
- Accounts Receivable: $40,000
- Inventory: $20,000
- Prepaid Expenses: $5,000
- Property, Plant, and Equipment: $200,000
- Accumulated Depreciation: -$10,000
- **Total Assets: $285,000**

Liabilities:

- Accounts Payable: $15,000
- Short-Term Loans: $10,000
- Long-Term Loans: $50,000
- Accrued Expenses: $7,000
- Income Tax Payable: $5,000
- Total Liabilities: $87,000

Equity:

- Owner's Capital: $200,000
- Retained Earnings: $-2,000
- Total Equity: $198,000
- Total Liabilities and Equity: $285,000

Cash Flow Statement for the Year Ended December 31, 20XX:

3. Yaml

Operating Activities:

- Net Income: $48,000
- Adjustments for:
- Depreciation: $10,000
- Changes in Working Capital:
- Increase in Accounts Receivable: -$10,000
- Increase in Inventory: -$5,000
- Increase in Accounts Payable: $2,000
- Interest Paid: -$8,000

- Income Tax Paid: -$20,000
- Net Cash Provided by Operating Activities: $17,000

Investing Activities:

- Purchase of Property, Plant, and Equipment: -$50,000
- Net Cash Used in Investing Activities: -$50,000

Financing Activities:

- Owner's Capital Investment: $30,000
- Short-Term Loan Proceeds: $10,000
- Long-Term Loan Repayment: -$20,000
- Net Cash Provided by Financing Activities: $20,000
- Net Increase in Cash: $-13,000
- Cash and Cash Equivalents, Beginning of Year: $43,000
- Cash and Cash Equivalents, End of Year: $30,000

Please note that these are simplified financial statements for illustrative purposes. In a real-world setting, financial statements would typically include more details and be subject to accounting and regulatory standards. Additionally, these figures are entirely fictional and do not represent any real business.

Legal and Regulatory Resources

Legal and regulatory compliance is crucial for businesses to operate smoothly and avoid legal issues. Here are some valuable legal and regulatory resources that can help you navigate the complex legal landscape:

1. **Local Business Regulatory Agencies:**
   - Local government websites, such as your city or county's official site, can provide information on local regulations, permits, and licenses that your business may require.
2. **Small Business Administration (SBA):**
   - The SBA provides a wealth of resources and guides on business regulations, compliance, and permits in the United States.
3. **U.S. Securities and Exchange Commission (SEC):**
   - If your business deals with securities or investments, the SEC offers information on regulations and compliance for publicly traded companies.

4. **Internal Revenue Service (IRS):**
   - The IRS website provides information on federal tax requirements, employer identification numbers (EIN), and tax forms.
5. **Occupational Safety and Health Administration (OSHA):**
   - OSHA's website contains resources on workplace safety regulations, standards, and compliance information.
6. **Environmental Protection Agency (EPA):**
   - If your business has environmental concerns, the EPA offers guidance on environmental regulations and permits.
7. **U.S. Patent and Trademark Office (USPTO):**
   - If you need to protect intellectual property, the USPTO provides information on patents, trademarks, and copyrights.
8. **Federal Trade Commission (FTC):**
   - The FTC provides guidance on consumer protection laws, advertising regulations, and antitrust laws.
9. **State and Local Chambers of Commerce:**
   - Chambers of Commerce often provide information and resources related to local regulations and compliance requirements.
10. **SCORE (Service Corps of Retired Executives):**
    - SCORE offers free mentoring and workshops, including legal advice, for small businesses and startups.
11. **LegalZoom and Rocket Lawyer:**
    - These online legal services offer a variety of legal document templates, resources, and affordable consultations with attorneys.
12. **FindLaw:**
    - FindLaw offers a wide range of legal resources, including articles, forms, and guides, to help you understand various legal topics.
13. **State-specific resources:**
    - Many states have their own regulatory agencies, such as the Department of Business Regulation or the Department of Commerce. These agencies provide information and support for state-specific regulations.
14. **Trade Associations and Industry-Specific Resources:**

- Many industries have trade associations that provide regulatory guidance and updates. Consider joining relevant associations to stay informed.

15. Legal Consultation:

- It's often advisable to consult with an attorney who specializes in business law to ensure your business is fully compliant with federal, state, and local regulations.

Remember that legal and regulatory requirements can vary significantly by location, industry, and the nature of your business. Always seek professional advice when necessary, and keep updated on changes in laws and regulations that may affect your business.